MAGIC.
You are it. Be it.

Gary M. Douglas & Dr. Dain Heer

ACCESS
CONSCIOUSNESS®
PUBLISHING

Contents

Introduction

By Gary Douglas

I'm Gary Douglas, the founder of Access, an energy transformation system that provides people with tools they can use to remove their limitations and disabilities and create some pretty amazing and wonderful new possibilities for themselves.

I began exploring consciousness and energy and other aspects of this weird, wild, wacky world in 1990, after realizing that I wasn't happy with my life. I'd had the cars, I'd had the houses, I'd had the success, and I had reached a point where none of it meant anything to me. I had everything that was considered valuable in this reality—and it still wasn't enough.

Life, as I was experiencing it, was a lot of hard work, a lot of effort, a lot of trauma, drama, upset and intrigue—and not very much joy. I knew that there had to be more to life or else there was no reason to be alive. There had to be more than this reality was offering because there was nothing about it that was magical, joyful or expansive. I began to look for some answers, and that has led me down some pretty interesting paths. I started out thinking that I wanted to know how to find the magic in my life. I didn't realize at the time that magic is all around us; it's something we create. Even though some amazing things had shown up in my life, boom-boom-boom, as soon as I asked for them, I didn't see the magic I had created.

Since that time, I've learned to think differently about the universe and the consciousness and oneness that we all are, and the magic that is an intrinsic part of it. In so doing, I've been able to make some tremendous changes in my life and help other people to make changes in theirs as well.

When I was kid people would ask me, "What do you want to be when you grow up?"

> I'd say, "I want to be happy."
> They'd say, "No, no, no, son. What do you want to be when you grow up?"
> I'd say, "Happy."
> They'd say, "No, no. Do you want to be a doctor or a lawyer or an Indian chief?"
> I'd say, "Yeah, as long as I'm happy."

In these pages, my friend and co-author, Dain Heer, and I share processes and tools that bring within reach the magic of happiness—as well as anything else you wish to create. Our Access seminar on Magic, which we've taught in cities throughout the U.S.A., Costa Rica, New Zealand and Australia, forms the foundation for this book. Now, with an understanding of the true magic of life, happiness is real.

By Dr. Dain Heer

My name is Dain Heer. Prior to discovering Access, I may have seemed successful on the outside, but inside I was very unhappy with myself and my life. I was living with my girlfriend and working as a chiropractor in a small beach community near Santa Barbara. There were people who would have looked at my life and said it was perfect, and yet I was so intensely unhappy that every morning after my girlfriend left for work, I would lie in bed and cry. I didn't have any idea how to make my life work or create and accomplish all the dreams I'd had for so long.

I had tried probably twenty or thirty different processes and systems for improving my life, and certainly one of them should have made my life work, but I always kept running into a brick wall. I was beginning to feel desperate. I knew there had to be an answer, but I had no idea where to find it, and in the end, suicide seemed like the best available option. One day in great desperation I said, "Look, universe, you've got six months or I'm killing myself." I was tired of struggling.

A week later, I saw a small classified ad in the weekly paper saying, "Access. All of life comes to me with ease and joy and glory. Call Shannon."

> I said, "Ease and joy and glory? Pollyanna put a f---ing ad in the paper. F--- you!" and I threw the paper down.
> A week later, I saw the same ad. "Access. All of life comes to me with ease and joy and glory. Call Shannon."
> This time I didn't throw the paper down; I called Shannon and demanded, "What do you do?"
> She said, "Oh, I do this thing called Access. I put my hands on your head. It's a process called the Bars. It'll last from an hour to an hour and a half. At the worst, you'll feel like you

had a good massage, and at the best, your whole life will change."

In the back of my head, I was saying, "My whole life better change, or I'm f---ing killing myself."

I was skeptical but I decided to try it. Shannon came to my office and started the Bars. The moment she put her hands on my head, I started giggling like a little kid, and I continued to giggle like a child for the full duration of the session—one hour and fifteen minutes. After the session, I experienced the first sense of peace I'd had in two and half years. I got up from the massage table, and for the first time in my life, I remember truly knowing that everything was okay—everything always had been, and everything always would be.

That session saved my life. I started working with Shannon once a week, and every time we worked together, my life changed, and I could see it. I started waking up in the morning with a sense of joy and possibility instead of, "Geez, I can't wait until I'm off this planet."

Access has been an amazing gift to me, and through using its processes and tools, magic has shown up in my life. I now ask for things, and they show up—but the real magic is in the ability to have the joy that's possible, the joy that can be created, the joy life can be.

Sure, magic is about the fun of having the things you desire show up in your life, but in a much larger way, magic is about consciousness that is experienced, not as an addendum to your life or that's done instead of your life. Magic is about consciousness as your life. It's not about meditating in a cave, removed from life, in order to have consciousness. You should be functioning from consciousness every moment you're alive. When you do, your life becomes truly magical and there's nothing you can't create. That's the beauty of it.

In this book, we share many of the things we have learned about magic: tools, processes and possibilities that you can use for functioning as consciousness in every living, waking, breathing, intense moment that you have on the planet.

Magic

Chapter One

Creating Magic In Your Life

Contrary to what a lot of people think, magic is not about controlling or forecasting natural events, it's not about getting everything you want when you want it, and it's not about spells, rituals and tricks. There are many metaphysical systems that teach you tricks, like blowing on people and knocking them over. Knocking people over with the breath of life and those kinds of things are very interesting, but they don't have anything to do with consciousness and they don't have anything to do with the true magic of life, which is the ability to receive everything. The universe is an amazing, abundant place, in case you hadn't noticed.

Have you ever truly looked at a tree with its leaves on? It's so outrageously abundant. You have to consider: Does the universe ever spare anything? Does the universe ever say, *Oh, you know, we've got a leaf shortage right now. Could you go without, tree?* No. The universe gives the tree everything it has to offer and the tree receives it without reservation. And that's the magic.

Magic Is Not About Using Force And Effort

One of the things we will talk about in this book is learning to follow energy rather than trying to push it. Magic is not about using force and effort as a way of making things occur in your life.

Years ago I (Gary) was in real estate and I was closing one escrow per month. My escrows always closed on time. I couldn't have them close a few days late because I needed the money. I controlled, dominated and manipulated the banks, the loan officers, the escrow officers and the clients, and I got every escrow to close exactly when it was scheduled to close. During the eight years I was in real estate, I think I had only three escrows that did not close.

During this time period, I went to a real estate seminar and the instructor asked, "How many of you closed three escrows last year?" Everybody in the class put their hand up. Then he asked, "How many of you closed six?" Fewer than half of the people raised their hands. Next he asked, "How many of you closed nine?" Five people raised their hands. Finally he asked, "How many of you closed one or more per month?" There were two of us. I said to myself, "Whoa, I thought I was a failure, and I'm closing more escrows than anybody in this room. I'm cool!"

But I knew I did it by control, and control meant making sure that everything went exactly the way I wanted it to go. I was on top of everything. I never failed to call the escrow officer every day. I didn't know that 25 percent of houses that go into escrow don't close. I didn't know that 90 percent of the agents give the papers to the escrow officer and never talk to her again until the closing date. Huh? How can you control things if you don't talk to people every day? My point in bringing this up is to say that I was really good at control—and what I've had to learn over time is to not be in control, and instead to follow the energy.

Elephants

During the tsunami in Asia in 2004, there were no casualties among the elephants. Did you hear about that? Days ahead of the tsunami, the elephants got the information, *Something big is happening,* and they said, "We're not going to be here for it. We're big, we're bad, we can kick anybody's ass, and guess what? We're out of here! See you later!"

The elephants broke all of those cute little chains that people put on them to confine them. "Excuse me, I'm pulling that three-foot stake out of the ground now." Doink. "Bye!" Why is that? The elephants were willing to receive the information that was available. They were willing to receive what the universe was sharing with them, and they knew, "I don't stand a chance against a tsunami, especially staked to the ground. Okay, we're out of here." It's tough for an elephant to swim when he's staked to the ground.

Magic Is About Receiving

The point here is that magic is about receiving. If you have to control everything to make your life happen, how much energy does that require of you? All of it. And if you are busy controlling everything, how much does that limit what you can create and what you can receive? It limits you enormously. What most people create is based on the amount of energy they put into continually controlling things. But, what if you were to create from receiving?

Is there a finite amount to what you can receive? No, there isn't. You as an infinite being have the capacity to receive infinitely—and when you receive infinitely, magic can truly show up in your life. But to have the magic, you have to be willing to receive.

Acknowledge The Magic

One of the reasons people think they don't have any magic in their lives is because they discount it when it happens. They think, "I wish I could have _____," and it shows up. What do they do then? Do they acknowledge they are creating the magic? No. They say, "Oh, that was just a coincidence. That was serendipitous. It just happened." They say, "Oh, that was a fortuitous coming together of events that were way beyond my control, and it didn't have anything to do with me." They throw away the magical truth of it. Guess how much more magic shows up?

We recently worked with a songwriter friend, and one of the things we asked him to do was to look back at his life and to spot all of the places when he thought about something—and it showed up. Every time he spotted one of those magical incidents, we asked him to acknowledge that he had created it. When he did that, when he acknowledged the magic that he had created in the past, more and more of it started showing up in his day-to-day life. These days, when he gets together with somebody, they write a song and the next day it gets cut. Amazing possibilities are showing up for him.

This can happen for you as well. When in your life have you thought about something, or said, "I wish ____," and it showed up?

In our seminars on Magic, we ask participants to do this as a homework assignment: Look back over your life and write down every time you thought about something or asked for something—and it showed up, as if by magic. Then—and this is important—acknowledge that it wasn't a coincidence, it wasn't a serendipitous event, it wasn't a fortuitous incident or accident, it wasn't "just one of those things"—it was magic. You created it. Look at those times and acknowledge that you created them. Acknowledge it out loud, "Okay, I created those. Wow, am I cool that I could create that? What else is possible?"

Chapter Two

Oneness And Creation

The infinite Oneness that we truly have and are is the source of everything that we would consider magic. If you are truly able to be the Oneness, to have the Oneness, to create it, to generate it, and to function in it, then magical things start to show up in your life. You are one with the awareness of whatever it takes to create what you're looking for.

Creation tends to be misunderstood and gets quite a bad rap. It's not often explained in a way that people can understand it or do it. How do things get created? People say, "Well, you've got to do hard work." They pit their energy against the universe and they use force and effort to make things happen. But what about the times you have created something by thinking about it—and it just showed up? Wasn't that creation?

People who operate from the *you've got to do the hard work* school of

creating, say, "Okay, I want to have a car and all I can afford is this little Toyota, and I'd better not get air conditioning because that would be too much money." They put conditions on their creation, and with those conditions, they don't allow anything greater to show up.

When you're in Oneness you ask, "Hey, universe, what are the infinite possibilities of a cool car showing up?", and some nice elderly lady who's not driving any more and whose husband just passed away, tells you she has 1999 Buick with 6,000 miles that she will sell to you for $250. Wow, could you have ever come up with that in a million years? Well, no, not if you're using the step-by-step, hard-work method.

We'd like you to come out of the step-by-step, linear construct and into Oneness and simultaneity, where instead of saying, "I've got to save up for the next twenty-five years and then I'll have it," you ask, "Hey universe, could I have this?" And it's, "Yes, you can. Here you are!"

Chapter Three

The Human Perspective vs The Humanoid Perspective

We have two majorly different perspectives and ways of creating here on Planet Earth: we have the human perspective and the humanoid perspective. The human perspective is that force is the source of creation. Humans think you have to work hard and sweat in order to create things. This is not so for humanoids. Humanoids recognize their oneness with the universe, and they don't pit themselves against it.

What's Different About Them?

Our investigation into humans and humanoids began on a trip to Nashville. I (Gary) am always trying to figure out how to help get people out of their shit and what's limiting them, and the way I do this is to walk into their space and look at the maze. I find the route out of the maze, and then I can figure out how to resolve it.

Dain and I were in our seats on the plane and two women walked down the aisle and sat down in front of us. I said, "I wonder what it would take to free somebody like that," and I went into their heads. Dain said, "Don't go in! Don't go in!", but it was too late. I was in there going, "Uhhh," and Dain had to work on me for forty-five minutes to get me out of their universe. I was trying to find a way out, only there was none. Their maze was closed.

The ladies took off their jackets and put them over the seats in front of them, and when the stewardess came by and said, "Here's your lunch," they put it in their laps.

> When the stewardess asked, "Would you like a drink?" one of the ladies said, "Well, I have no place to put my drink."
> The stewardess said, "Put your tray table down."
> The lady said, "I don't have a tray table."
> The stewardess said, "See this man here sitting next to you? That thing down there, that's your tray table."
> The lady said, "I don't have one."
> The stewardess said, "If you will take your jacket off the back of the seat . . ."
> The lady said, "I'm not putting my jacket on the floor."

I was going, "Oh shit, how did I get in here? How do I get out?" It wasn't until I asked myself, "Okay, what's different about these people? How are they different from Dain and me and the people we work with in Access? What's different about them?" Then I got it: "They're so human." Doink. "Oh my God. We're different. We're not human. What are we? We're humanoid! I can't believe this. I've been thinking I'm human all this time and I'm not. I'm humanoid."

I got free by understanding that I wasn't one of them. It took the recognition that I wasn't like them. I have known people like that my whole life and I had always tried to understand where they were coming from. I hadn't realized there were two species of beings on planet Earth. This was very helpful information.

Humanoids Look For Ways To Make Things Better

Humans live in judgment of everybody else and think that life is just the way it is, and nothing is ever right, so don't even bother to think about another possibility. Humanoids, on the other hand, look for ways to make things better. If you invent things, if you search out things, if you are always looking for a better, bigger way of creating something, you're a humanoid. Humanoids are the people who create change. They create the inventions, the music and the poetry. They create all the things that come out of a lack of satisfaction with the status quo.

This Is All There Is

I (Gary) talked to my stepdad, who was very definitely human, after he had a heart attack. I said, "Dad, what was it like for you having that heart attack?" Nobody had asked him that question.

> He said, "Well, I remember having the heart attack and standing outside my body looking at it . . ." He trailed off and then started over again.
> "Well, I had the heart attack and then I saw them putting the

electrodes on my chest . . ." Again, he stopped mid-sentence, waited a moment, and then started over again.

"Well," he finally said, "I had the heart attack and then they put the electrodes on my chest and they zapped me."

He could not have a reality in which he was out of his body watching these things occur. It was a great example of what happens to people when they can't have what doesn't fit their judgments of reality. His reality was that you are a body and that's all there is. A human can never have anything that doesn't match their viewpoint, "This is all there is." Humans are the people who do not believe in reincarnation. They do not believe in other possibilities. They do not believe in miracles or magic. The doctors and the lawyers and the Indian chiefs create everything. Humans create nothing.

Forty-seven percent of the population is humanoid, and they are the creators of everything that changes in this reality. Fifty-two percent is human. (And the final 1 percent? Some day we'll tell you about them!) Humans hold onto things the way they are and never want anything to change. Have you ever been to somebody's house where they haven't changed the furniture in thirty years? Human.

Humanoids Tend To Judge Themselves

One of the big differences between humans and humanoids is that humanoids tend to judge themselves, whereas humans judge others. You may, as a humanoid, occasionally try to judge others, but usually you only do that when trying to make yourself more like humans. Judging others is hard work for you. Most humanoids find it impossible. When they hear a judgment of someone, they say, "Huh? That would be important based on what? So-and-so did that? Well, maybe under certain circumstances so would I." A human, on the other hand, will say with great certainty, "No, I would never do that."

Instead of sitting in judgment of others, humanoids tend to sit in judgment of themselves. They find fault with themselves. They try to figure out how to make themselves better. A human doesn't do this. A human will tell you what's wrong with you, and how if you just did things differently or if you would just get in line with everybody else, everything would be okay. "If you'd just stop doing all those weird things you do," they say, "you'd be just fine. And why would you want anything better than what you've got, anyway, because this is all there is?" That's pretty much their defining point of view.

The idea of bringing up this human/humanoid thing is not about sitting in judgment of humans. It's about becoming aware that we humanoids are a different species with an infinite capacity to create magic and miracles. It's important to know this so we can let go of our propensity to judge ourselves and buy into the limited human perspective that is all around us.

Chapter Four

What Is Living In The Question?

Humanoids create by living in the question. They recognize their oneness with the universe and they know that the universe will provide infinitely—if they ask and they're willing to listen and receive. Living in the question means using questions to bypass the limited answers your mind provides. The more you live in the question, the more infinite possibilities will show up for you. You can bypass 90 percent of the steps that humans have to go through to create something when you are willing to have the magic and live in the question.

What Would It Take For ____ To Show Up?

When you live in the question, you ask a question to create an invitation. When you ask a question like *What would it take for ____ to show up?* the universe will give you opportunities for that to happen.

Recently I went to take some money out of my savings account because I didn't seem to have enough money. I was saying, "Damn it! Why don't I have enough money? I don't understand this! What's it going to take for more money to show up? It's ridiculous that I don't have enough money. What's it going to take?"

The next day, I took my briefcase, which I hadn't used for about three months, out of the closet and there was $1,600 in cash that I had stowed away for some reason. Two days after that, Dain and I flew to Florida, and when we got there, our friend Jill handed Dain an envelope and said,

> "This was with the credit card machine."
> Dain asked, "What is it?"
> She said, "Checks that were never cashed from a class you and Gary did."

There were $2,000 worth of checks in it.

The same day I got a call from a lady whose credit card hadn't been charged for $1,800 worth of services, and a day later, I found a check for $500 in a drawer where I'd left it.

That was the $6,000 I'd taken out of my savings account. I said, "Hmm. I guess I wasn't short of money. I just wasn't looking."

The funny thing is, money is still flowing in. I had a lady call me today and say,

> "You know that class I took a couple of months ago? They didn't charge my account for it. I'm mailing you a check."
> I said, "Okay, cool! How does it get any better than this?"

You Have To Ask A Question

You have to ask a question for the universe to give you an answer. You have to ask. It's no good to say, I want more money. That only means I lack of more money—and there's no question in it. Always use a question: *What would it take for ____ to show up?*

One of the great truths of the Bible is ask and you shall receive. The problem is that most people ask for limitations rather than possibilities.

"I've Got To Have This" Is Not A Question

"I've got to have this" is not a question. Have you ever noticed that the things you decide you've got to have end up being out of your reach for long periods of time? But when you ask *What's the possibility of ____ showing up?* Boom! It's: *Wow, that was an amazing coincidence. I ran into the right person at just the right time!*

These so-called accidents or coincidences, these serendipitous things that happen, are not fate or destiny. They are examples of your capacity to create and manifest instantaneously.

How Does It Get Any Better Than This?
What Are The Infinite Possibilities?

A friend of ours who is in real estate has been applying these principles and using questions like *How does it get any better than this?* and *What are the infinite possibilities?*, and lately he's been getting calls for increasingly more expensive properties.

He doesn't categorize himself in what he does. He remains open to the infinite possibilities. Most realtors categorize themselves with, "I only do single-family residences," or "I only do commercial," or "I only do this or that."

The *only* is a linear construct of the human perspective. Humans think you have to specialize. They say things like, "If you don't specialize, nobody will do anything with you." Wrong. When you are open to the universe and the infinite possibilities—*anything* can happen.

Stop Functioning From A Linear Construct

In order to have the magic of your life, we have to stop functioning from a linear construct. It's not: *I don't have any money. I've got to borrow some from so-and-so.* It's: *Okay, so what's it going to take for the money to show up in my life? I know it's going to happen. What's it going to take for it to show up? And won't it be interesting to see how it shows up?*

When you use a linear construct like, *Oh, I've got to borrow it from somebody,* you've defined and limited the only way it can come to you. What if you don't have anybody willing to loan you the money? What if they're looking to borrow it from you that particular week?

But if you live in the question, you can do something different. Instead of saying, *Okay, I'd like to have this money. Whom am I going to borrow it from?*, ask, *Hey, what are the infinite possibilities of the money showing up in my life?*

Do you see how the second approach is more expansive? When you function from expansiveness and possibilities, those are what show up. The more you live in the question, the more possibilities begin to appear.

We've all grown up with human points of view which taught us that we have to function in the linearity of reality. What if that is not the truth of you? What if the truth of you is something completely different—and all you have to do is be willing to let it show up?

Most people have been taught that they have to do in order to have and in order to be. So would you like to give up that crock of shit right now? Recognize that doing, being and having can come from a totally non-linear point of view.

Have You Ever Asked For Something . . . And It Showed Up A Year Later?

Have you ever asked for something, then forgotten that you asked for it, and it showed up a year later? And you said, I was thinking about this a year ago! You asked for it and then the universe rearranged itself to have that thing show up. If you truly ask for something and know that you'll get it, it will show up for you.

It's not about controlling when it shows up. It's about allowing it to show up and being willing to receive it when it does. We ask for a million dollars today, and if we don't receive it by tomorrow, we figure we have failed and the asking stuff doesn't work. Or we decide we're bad at asking. Or we decide we aren't going to receive what we asked for because it didn't come instantaneously the way we thought it ought to, or from the direction we thought it had to come from. We decide the only answer we're going to get is, No, you can't have that, which is a terrible mistake. When you ask for something, the universe has to start rearranging things. You're not the only person who's asking for something, you know!

So, start exercising your humanoid perspective and create by living in the question. Recognize your oneness with the universe—don't pit yourself against it. Use unlimited questions and be willing to receive the unlimited possibilities when they show up.

Three of the questions you can ask the universe are:

- How Does It Get Any Better Than This?
- What Are the Infinite Possibilities?
- What Would It Take for ＿＿＿ to Show Up?

Chapter Five

Magic Is
"Ask And Receive"

The simple truth of magic is: ask and receive. It's very light. You ask, but you don't put a lot of attention on it and you don't put a lot of intention on it. *Attention* is the point of view that you have an obstacle to overcome, so you'd better focus on it. You'd better put your attention on what you've asked for, to try and make it happen. *Intention* is the idea that there is an obstacle that you have to overcome, so you have to use a lot of force to make it show up.

Have you ever tried to create something and it wasn't showing up the way you knew damn well that it should, and you started feeling heavier and heavier? Someone might come up and say, "Hi, how are you doing?" and you'd say, "Get out of my way! I'm creating! Go away!"

Something like this happened to us. We taught a series of great Access seminars in Australia and people experienced tremendous change and transformation. We were really pleased and when we got to the airport, we decided, "Okay, we're such powerful creators, we deserve to ride business class on the way home. We're going to fly in business class." (Notice that we weren't asking? You don't hear any haughtiness in our approach, do you?)

We decided we were going to fly business class, and that we were going to get an upgrade. We went up to the counter, and Dain said, "Hi. Do you have any upgrades available for grand and glorious creators?" The answer was, "No."

Okay, I thought, *I've got billions of miles on United.* I decided to call United and find out how to get an upgrade from them. They said, "Sorry, you can't get an upgrade on a different carrier." We couldn't buy an upgrade, we couldn't force one with miles and we couldn't smile and flirt into an upgrade because the people we were trying to smile and flirt with were beyond smiling and flirting.

"Okay," we said, "we'll take our flight to Auckland, and if they have any space, maybe they'll sell us an upgrade. We might have to pay a little more but no problem, right? They used to do this for $250."

We got to Auckland and went up to the service desk and the lady said, "No."

We asked, "Why?"

She said, "No."

We asked, "Could we buy one?"

She said, "No."

We were disheartened because we had already decided that we were such grand and glorious creators that we deserved an upgrade and that we were going to get upgraded. Hello! The universe should be providing us with an upgrade.

Finally we said, "Wait a minute. Is there something we're not looking at here?" (Notice that we finally asked a question?) After we heard no eight hundred times, we began to think, *Gee, there may be something we're not looking at here.*

We were standing around in the airport, getting pissed off at the people who were getting upgraded, and suddenly we realized, "We're not really doing what we talked about and taught, are we? No, we're not. So what are we not looking at?" Then we got it: We asked, "What are the infinite possibilities of having a great trip regardless of where the heck we sit?" Everything started feeling lighter all of a sudden.

Once we finally got around to asking, "Okay, what are the infinite possibilities of having a great trip?", we realized, "Hey, we get to hang out together the whole way home." It turned out that we got seats next to each other and there was an open seat next to us, so we had plenty of room to spread out and we had a great trip, just by changing our point of view and being willing to receive what was actually being given, instead of deciding that we had to receive business-class upgrades to show what grand and glorious creators we were.

Have you ever decided that you *had* to have the equivalent of a business-class upgrade? Or that you had to have your whole life unfold the way you decided that it had to because, if you didn't get it exactly the way you wanted it, it meant you were a friggin' loser? Why not let go of that for a moment and think about receiving what the universe is offering you? You could be surprised. It might make you feel lighter. You might discover that you're having a much better time.

Chapter Six

Pico Universes vs. True Creation

Have you ever heard of Walter Mitty? He was the hero of a short story about a meek, henpecked guy with a domineering wife and a boring, lousy job. He lived in an imaginary world and created extravagant scenarios about being a daring surgeon, a heroic pilot and a dashing naval commander. Most of us, in some way or another, are Walter Mittys. We take a grain of sand and create entire universes about what it's going to mean and our role in it.

Did you ever daydream when you were a kid? Have you ever created a whole universe that existed in your head? That's a pico universe. It's a small, private universe of your own. Every time you go into a daydream, you go into pico universe. You don't want to be present anymore—and a pico universe is a way of escaping the present. You decide, *This is so friggin' boring that I don't want to be here anymore,* and off you go, into the pico universe.

We create a pico universe when we take some small event or comment and say, *Oh, that means . . .* We create a universe about what something is going to look like.

Shortly after I (Gary) got divorced, I went out with a lady and we had a really good time together. I went home, and as I was standing in the shower, I was thinking, "Oh gosh, that was wonderful. She's really nice. I wonder what it would be like to have sex with her? I think it would be fun. I wonder if she's the one."

The one? I'd been out with her once and there I was standing in the shower creating her as the love of my life. I was creating a pico universe about our future together and I didn't even know her last name. Is that a little insane or what?

What If . . . ?

Have you ever had the experience of getting a really great idea, deciding you wanted to create something and in your mind going through exactly what it was going to look like? And then you never actually did anything with it? *What if . . . ? What if . . . ? What if . . . ?* Those are pico universes. We create a pretense of what it's going to be. It's a form of creation. We create the whole thing in our minds. We complete it in our imaginations without ever actually doing anything. Why don't the universes we create in this way show up in the physical universe? Because we've already completed them in our heads.

We've worked with a number of people who have had problems with obesity and we've found it was very effective for them to do some kind of movement.

> I (Gary) asked one lady who was obese, "What kind of
> movement would your body like to do?"
> She said, "My body would like to dance."

A couple of months later when I saw her, she had even more weight on her body.

> I asked her, "What's going on?"
> She said, "Well, I think about dancing and I think about the
> music and the steps I'll do and what it's going to feel like and
> how great it's going to be—and then I never do it."
> I said, "Yeah, because you complete it all in your head. You
> create a pico universe about what it is going to be like and
> you never actually do it."

Is that living in the present? No.

How Do You Stop Doing Walter Mitty-isms?

The way you stop doing Walter Mitty-isms is by not allowing yourself to create pico universes. Instead of thinking about something or imagining what it's going to be like, simply ask yourself, *Okay, what's this going to look like?* Then you *do* it.

If you ask yourself, *Who am I today and what grand and glorious adventure am I going to have?*, it puts you in the state of being willing to see your life as a present-time adventure instead of a future possibility.

Sometimes people ask us what to do about their runaway brains. They want to allow the universe to create for them. They're trying to align with the universe and create things by living in the question—but their brains are running off in a completely different direction, constructing answers and pico universes. When that happens, you have to recognize, *Oh, I just went out of the question.* Live in the question, not the answer.

Have You Created Pico Universes Instead Of Creating Your Own Life?

Have you created pico universes instead of creating your own life? Everything you've done to create pico universes, and all the talent and ability you have put into the creation of pico universes instead of actually being in your own life, would you destroy and uncreate it please?

It's really about being in the present. When you are willing to live in the present and you are not functioning from the past, it's harder to create pico universes. When you've got a past that tells you exactly who, what, where, when, why and how you are, and exactly how to respond in any situation or circumstance, you start to function from rules and limitations: *When they do this, I'll do this.* When you have all of this stuff backed up behind you as though it's the source of creation for you, there's no such thing as living in the question. In fact, there are no questions; there are only answers. You attempt to create your life based on limited answers and limited, linear points of view.

Your Imagination Is A Limitation

Even your imagination is a limitation, because imagination is a function of the mind. Your imagination can only define what you already know—just as your mind can only define what you already know. Imagination cannot imagine beyond the limits of what you have already decided exists. In terms of infinite beingness and infinite knowing, perceiving and receiving, your imagination is a limitation. It is not awareness.

Imagination and awareness are sometimes confused. As a child you may have had awarenesses about things, and your parents might have said, "Oh, that's just your imagination." They were training you to be normal, average and real. They were training you to be sane and normal so that you would be like everybody else. It didn't work, though, did it?

Normal and *average* and *real* are actually huge limitations because they don't allow for the greatness of you. They don't allow for the infinite possibilities available to you in this universe. Have you ever used force and effort against yourself in order to make yourself appear normal, average and real, just like everybody else? Would you like to give that up now?

Who Are You Today And What Grand And Glorious Adventure Are You Going To Have?

What would happen if you gave up being a Walter Mitty and began to create your life in the present rather than inhabiting the pico universes in your head? Are you ready to see your life as a present-time adventure instead of a future possibility? Who are you today and what grand and glorious adventures are you going to have?

Chapter Seven

Excitement And Fear

Most of us have, at one time or another, misidentified or misapplied *excitement* as *fear.* When I was a little kid, I (Gary) was at an amusement park and was about to go on a ride. I was really excited. My mom looked at me and said, "Now don't be afraid, dear." I thought, "Oh, this is fear that I'm feeling. Okay." So every time after that when excitement would come up, I thought it was fear. It wasn't until the first time I had sex that I realized excitement wasn't the same thing as fear.

Sometimes getting excited about something before it happens is pico futures or pico universes. It's one of those places where you take a little grain of sand and say, *Oh, I'm so excited about this. It's going to be so great. It's going to be like this . . .*

When Dain and I do classes, I never go in with the idea that I'm excited about the class. I go in with, *Okay, I wonder what we're going to do today. I wonder what this is going to look like and whether things will go in the direction I think they should.*

We know that the people who attend our classes create the class. We don't. It's the same with everything else in our lives. The people we are involved with create our lives with us. When we anticipate, we create a pico future so that we can control the outcome. We think *If I create with enough force and effort, it will turn out to be as wonderful as I have decided it's going to be.*

Have you ever planned one of those vacations where you have it all figured out? You were going to stay here, you were going to stay there, and everything was arranged. You were so excited about going on this vacation. Then you got there and said, *Okay, now what am I going to do? I'm bored to tears.* The anticipation and the excitement happened before you got there. You had the vacation in the planning of it. You shouldn't have bothered to actually go on it.

Have you ever taken on a road trip where you had no clue where you were going to stay or what was going to happen, and it turned out to be really fun? That's because you were living in the moment, not by the plan.

We love the story of a friend's dad who went on a road trip. He drove through eight states without stopping because he kept thinking something better was going to happen.

Our friend would ask, "Dad, can we stop here and see this?"
His dad would say, "No, we've got to get there."
Our friend would ask, "Dad, can we stop there and do that?"
His dad would say, "No, we've got to get there."

Some people spend their whole lives waiting to get there instead of having fun while they're on the road. When we do that, we eliminate our joy of the moment. We never go on the journey because of the anticipation of getting there.

Chapter Eight

How Do You Create What You'd Like To Have?

Get The Feeling Of What It Would Be Like To Have It

Here is the way to create what you'd like to have: First, get the feeling of what it would be like to have it. If you'd like to have a new car, ask yourself, *What kind of car is going to feel really wonderful to drive? What's going to make my life exciting when I drive?* Get the image of what it would be like. By image, we mean the feel of it. What would it feel like to drive this car?

Did you pick your car based on the utility of it? Do you spend hours driving in bumper-to-bumper traffic, thinking *My car gets me everywhere I want to go. It's a good, sturdy, reliable car.*

Well, I (Gary) don't like sturdy, reliable cars. I want something that's fun. For me, if it ain't fun, I don't want to do it. I want to feel excited about the car I drive. I want to enjoy driving it.

Getting the feeling of what you want is different from creating a pico universe. If you were turning it into a pico universe, you'd be saying, *Oh, it will be so good to have it because then I'll have this—and then I'll have this—and then I'll have this.* You'd be saying, *Well, having it will mean that I can do that, and that will mean . . . and that will mean . . .* Whenever you put meaning, form or structure onto it, you create a limitation. That's different from asking, Okay, I'd like a car that does this, and has this, and what are the infinite possibilities of something like that showing up in my life?

When I (Gary) decided that I wanted to get a car for my daughter, I knew I wanted a car that got good gas mileage so she could afford to fill it up, because I wanted her to learn how to take responsibility for her own car. I asked, *What kind of car can I get her that she would like, and that I would enjoy driving when she was using my Tahoe?* I said *I want a Beamer convertible.* So, I started looking for Beamer convertibles in a certain price range and age range and I found something that was a good deal, but was a bit older than what I'd thought I wanted. I knew it was the right car, though, and I bought it.

It's had an amazing number of problems, none of which were permanent, and all of which came from people treating it with neglect. The mechanic said, "This is an awesome car. Once you get all this stuff fixed, it's going to be a great car." Other people weren't willing to take the time, energy or money to fix it, but I was. This car wanted to be taken care of. It wanted to be loved. It wanted to be admired. And it's getting admired. It's getting loved. It's a hot little '99 M3 convertible. My kid loves it. She got a ticket for speeding at ninety-five miles per hour.

Isn't that interesting? I did not ask for a car that was mechanically perfect. I left certain parameters out of my image. I didn't say *It's got to be in good shape and it's got to have been well taken care of.* Those were not things I asked for. I asked for a car that was fun, good looking, in this price range and in this category. Later, with another car I bought, I said *It's got to be in great shape,* and that's exactly what I got. But not with this one. So, I learned a lesson. Ten seconds of unconsciousness can only cost you a billion years of pain and suffering—or $7,000 in repairs.

We tend to decide what we would like to have, but often we don't include what we don't want. Dain and I know a guy who listed all the traits that he wanted in a woman. He said, "I want her to have this, this, this and this," but he forgot to add what he didn't want. He forgot to make his list of not-wants. He ended up marrying a woman who had all the traits he asked for, but he also got all the traits that he hated in a woman and forgot to mention.

Sometimes, however, when you get something you think you don't want, it may actually be something you desire, especially if you're living in the question. A friend of ours was flying from Phoenix to Los Angeles. Before she got on the plane she thought about how difficult it was going to be to carry her two heavy bags from the airport to the car rental place. She was dreading it, but she decided she would be able to handle it and let it go.

When she got to the baggage claim in Los Angeles, she realized that one of her bags hadn't arrived. She asked, "What's right about this I'm not getting?" She went into the claim department, got a rental car, and drove up to Santa Barbara. The next day FedEx delivered her bag to her. She was dreading having to carry two heavy bags around the airport, so the airline lost her bag and it was delivered to her by FedEx. How does it get any better than that?

When you're functioning from the magic you truly are, and you think, *Gee, I really don't want to have to carry those bags,* that's the way things can happen for you. You don't have to carry them. They disappear and then somebody else brings them to you. You create what you ask for.

Lightly State Your Desire

When you decide you are going to do something in your life, it's amazing how quickly it will show up, and the way it will show up. After you have gotten the feeling of what it would be like to have what you desire, lightly state your request or your target or your desire. Say, *I'd like to do this.* Then, ask *What is it going to take for that to show up in my life?* Part of creating magic is asking the right question. You express a commitment to creating something in your life, you ask a question and you're not vested in the outcome. It's light.

Years ago I (Gary) saw a video of this guy channeling an entity named Bashar. I looked at it and I said, *How come he can do that and I can't? He's no taller than I am. He certainly doesn't speak any better English than I do. He's no better looking than I am. I don't know what any of those things have relevance to, but how come he can do it and I can't?* I didn't think about it again. Three years later it happened. I began to channel Rasputin.

I'd like to do that is a request. I didn't put a time limit on it, and it took a while for the universe to twist things around in my world to the point where I was available for that. Every time you make a request, you create the possibility. You lightly make your request and that's it.

Ask For A Little Help

Oftentimes, in order to get the result you desire, you have to be willing to receive a little help. Ask the consciousness of the universe to help you create the thing you desire. Many people never think of asking the consciousness of the universe to help them. Why is that?

Most of us have gone to great trouble to set up our lives so we don't have to ask for help. If you don't ask, you can't be disappointed, right? We pretend we're not asking and then we're disappointed because what we wished for didn't manifest. We might even think we didn't manifest it because there's something wrong with us.

If you request of the universe what you desire, the universe will give it to you. But you can't be vested in the outcome, nor can you be vested in when it shows up. A vested point of view is: *It's got to turn out this way. It has to come to fruition by such-and-such a date. It's got to produce this and if it doesn't, then my life sucks.*

Don't Be Vested In The Outcome

Being vested in the outcome is when you say, *I've got to have a 2002 BMW M3 for $10,000 and it's got to have no miles on it and it's got to have $2,000 wheels on it and it's got to look like this.* Being vested in the time frame is, I've got to have $10,000 by the end of the month! Are these requests? No. Is there any lightness in them? No.

Humans create from decision, force, effort, violence and judgment, whereas humanoids create by requesting things and getting the feeling of what they desire. You say, *I wonder what it would be like for this to happen.* Poof. It shows up. *I wonder what it would be like for that to show up in my life.* Boom. There it is. You request of the universe what you desire, and the universe gives it to you.

It's not a decision that is cast in concrete. It's not: *I'm going to do this! I've got to do this! I need to do this! This is what I deserve!* No. It's light. *There is no effort or force behind it. I'd like to do this. What is it going to take for that to show up in my life?*

I (Gary) have a friend who decided that he was going to have sex with a certain lady. She was flirting outrageously with him and they went out for drinks and he said,

> "I don't do relationships. I'm interested in sex."
> She said, "Well, that's wonderful. I just got out of a relationship and I know I'll get a good one some day soon."
> At the end of the evening he said, "Would you like to come up to my room?" She said, "Oh yeah, that would be great."

His point of view was he told her he was interested in sex. Was he vested in the outcome? Yes. She put out that she wanted another good relationship. Was she vested in the outcome? Yes. She wanted relationship. He wanted sex.

> So they got up to the room and she said, "No, no. I don't want to have sex. Just hold me all night long."
> He said, "Okay, I'll hold you, because I really never wanted to have sex. All I wanted to do is hold you."

As a result, he was pissed off the next day.

> I asked him, "Why didn't you say, 'No. Go home'?"
> He said, "I can do that?"
> I said, "Yeah. You can say no."

He said, "I can?"

I said, "Sure. It's not just women who can say no. Men can say no, too."

He was so vested in how it was going to work out (sex) that he wasn't willing to hear her point of view (relationship). She was so attached to the outcome she wanted (relationship) that she wasn't willing to hear his point of view (sex). Neither one of them got what they wanted.

She looked at him and thought, "This man will be perfect for me."

He looked at her and thought, "She'll have sex with me. It'll be fun."

Were either of them listening to the other? No. Each of them was vested in their point of view. They each made a decision that kept them from looking into the other person's universe and seeing what was available.

If you're vested in your point of view, whatever it is you're asking for isn't going to happen.

How would this play out if you weren't invested in the outcome? Let's say you're interested in having a relationship. You'd meet someone. You'd have the awareness of being attracted to that person. *He/she's really cute.* You'd have the awareness that he/she had certain qualities you desired. *He/she's really smart and has a wonderful sense of humor.* And then you would be in the question, *Is he/she available for what I'm looking for?*

This is different from: *I want a relationship. This person fits all of my categories, therefore he/she must be available for what I desire. Anybody who fits all my categories must be available for what I desire.* Can you see how being vested in the outcome is far different from being present, aware, and in the question?

When you go into a business meeting, do you go with the idea that you must get a particular result? Or are you open to what is possible? If you go without a specific result you have to achieve, you can find out what is possible, and what tends to show up is even more than you were going to ask for in the first place.

When you get the idea *This is what the result is going to be,* you have become vested in the outcome. You stop seeing what is possible and only see the result you've decided on. What inevitably occurs is less than what is possible.

Why is this? You've made a judgment about what's necessary, and when you make a judgment, you are unable to see anything that doesn't fit into it. Decisions and judgments always exclude anything that doesn't match them. You can't see anything that doesn't match what you've already decided or judged is going to be the result. You end up creating limitations instead of possibilities. Instead, go in with the idea, *I wonder what's possible here.* Go in with a question.

When Magic Occurs, Acknowledge You Created It

The final step of creating what you'd like to have is acknowledging what you've created. You've got to acknowledge the magic every time, *Oh, wow, that's cool. Isn't this great?* Acknowledge what you created—and then go back to the question: *How did I create that? How do I get more of that? How does it get any better than this?*

How Do You Create What You'd Like To Have?

The steps to follow in order to create what you'd like to have are:

- Get the feeling of what it would be like to have it.

- Lightly state your desire.

- Ask for a little help.

- Don't be vested in the outcome.

- When the magic occurs, acknowledge that you created it.

- Go back to the question.

Chapter Nine

What Else Is Possible?

Dain has been such a gift to me (Gary) as a friend and collaborator because he's always asking, "What else is possible?" When something comes up, he'll work it out and then he'll say, "Okay, now that that's clear, what else is there?" He never stops looking for what else is possible.

Do you remember when you were a kid and you approached life with questions like, *Okay, what else can we do? Whoa, that was fun. What else is possible?* That was the whole idea. You were open to every new possibility. Every day was exciting. Your childhood was magical in that regard, until somewhere between five or ten years old, something happened and you began to be less than enthusiastic about the possibilities.

We'd like to re-introduce you to enthusiasm for life. It starts with asking questions like, *Okay, so what else is possible for today? What else can we do?*

The magic in your life is created from the true magic of you, which is the presence of you. That's the thing you had when you were a kid that you think you don't have now. When you were a little kid, you were willing to just be you. That was it. You didn't try to do anything else. You weren't out to impress anybody. You just were you.

When you were a kid, did you wake up in the morning and hit the snooze alarm twenty-seven times before you got up? Hell no. You were up at six in the morning, and your parents would say, "Would you please go back to sleep? Thank God it's Saturday morning. Go watch some cartoons, would you?"

You'd say, *Okay, I'll go watch some cartoons. Oh wow, those cartoons are cool. Want to go outside and play? Okay, that was fun. Want to eat something? Cool. Okay, that was enough food. What else do you want to do?*

What if you lived your life like that? *Okay, What else is possible?*

Chapter Ten

There's Consciousness In Everything

There's consciousness in everything. There is consciousness in rocks and cars, in houses and furniture, not to mention musical instruments, plants and things of beauty. All things have consciousness, and if you ask them, they will tell you where they want to go and whom they want to belong to.

Your House Knows Who It Wants To Live In It

Your house knows who it wants to live in it. There's a vibration that feels good to it. When the right people come in to your house, it will go *Oh, these people have the right vibration.* Have you ever met someone for the first time and instantaneously felt a connection with him or her? You think, *Oh, I really like this person!* That's because you're energetically connected and energetically present with them and none of the usual barriers exist. The same thing can happen when you have something that's selling itself. People will say, *Oh, I like this. I feel good being in this house. . . I really like this jacket. . . I really like this car. . . I like this song. It turns me on.*

Your creations and possessions have a consciousness and a life of their own. You can tell them, *Hey, pull energy into yourself. Pull energy to you and through you from everyone and everything that's going to be looking for you. Then send a little trickle out to all those people who are looking for you and can't find you, and when they show up, equalize the flow.*

I (Gary) told a version of this to some friends who were real estate agents. I said, "Okay, pull energy into the house from all over the universe and let little trickles go out to all those people who are looking for this house and don't know it. Then ask the house, when people come in, to equalize the flow."

They did that and they started selling every open house they had. That's unheard of; it doesn't often happen in real estate. Rarely do sellers ever sell at an open house, but they did.

Some other friends used this to sell their home even before it was listed. They had found another house they wanted to buy. They made an offer on it, and the owners accepted their offer, but they said, "We won't wait more than thirty days for you to sell your current place. If you want this house, you have to sign a sales contract without any contingencies."

They called us and asked, "What should we do?"

We told them to pull energy into their current house from all over the universe and let little trickles go out to all the people that were looking for it, and then ask the house to equalize the flow when they walked in the door.

They called us three days later and they said, "Right after we started doing that, we got a call from a realtor who said, 'Is there any chance your house is for sale because I've got some clients who are looking for exactly the kind of house you have.'" Not only that, but after they signed a contract with those people, someone else offered to buy it.

They told a friend of theirs about it, and he said, "Yeah, yeah, yeah, right. I don't believe in that magic shit."

Three months later, he called them asked, "What is that stuff you did to sell your house? Our house has been on the market for three months and no one has even come to look at it."

They said, "Okay, this is what you do," and they told him.

Within two weeks he had an offer on the house, and it sold within the month.

Gotta Sell The Caddy

When I (Gary) decided to sell my Cadillac, it sold itself. It was a 1971 Cadillac El Dorado convertible. Black with red leather interior. Beautiful car. It was never listed, never offered for sale anywhere. I just lightly said, *Gotta sell the Caddy*. Three days later my daughter was driving it, and somebody asked her,

> "Any chance your car is for sale?"
> She said, "Yes, my dad's going to sell it."
> He said, "How much?"

She told him how much she thought it was. The potential buyer took the telephone number, called his friend in northern California who had been looking for a car like mine forever, and the guy came down and bought it. Doink.

You pull the energy, let a little trickle of it go back to all the people in the universe who are looking for it and when they show up, you equalize the energy. You ask the product or the house or the car or whatever you're selling to equalize the flow—to let the energy flow freely in both directions—when the right person comes in.

It's the same with just about everything you own and create. These creations have consciousness and are actually willing to make choices. *Oh, I'm a song. Okay, cool. Who wants to hear me? Anybody want to hear me?* The song is saying, *Yes, I want to be heard. It is really cool for me to be heard.* Your house is saying, *I want to have somebody live in me that would feel good to have inside.*

If you're selling your house, give the consciousness in the house the job of selling itself. Don't assume you have a problem. You don't. First of all, it's not a problem, and second, the house can choose. The horse can choose. The car can choose.

It sounds funny to talk about empowering an apartment, or a house or a car, but when you empower something to function from consciousness, that's what it will do. The only ones on the planet who don't choose consciousness are humans and humanoids desperately seeking to be like them. Everything else functions from the consciousness it naturally is.

Hey, What Are You Doing Up There?

When I (Gary) asked my horse whom he wanted to belong to, he said he wanted Dain instead of me. So now he's Dain's horse, and Dain has to pay to feed him and to keep a home over his head. Does Dain own him? Or does he own Dain?

I got on the horse once to show Dain how to do something and the horse asked, "Hey, what are you doing up there?"

I said, "I just have to show him something."

He started acting up and I said, "Hey, just let me show him how to do this, okay? I just want to show him how to do it and I'll get off."

The horse went around the ring three times and he said, "Okay, get off. Dain knows what you want to show him now," and he stopped like that. Done. Get off. Okay, fine. It was a very new way of riding a horse for me. I always had the point of view I was in control. I was very silly.

Get Rid Of Me

I (Dain) had a car with a transmission problem. The transmission was broken and the car was saying, "Get rid of me. It's time for us to part, damn it." But I loved my car so much. It was an Eclipse.

I took it to the mechanic and he said, "Look, you need to get rid of this thing now. It's going to cost between one and two grand to fix it, and the car is only worth about six." But I didn't want to get rid of it, and I didn't want sell it to somebody else if it had a major problem, so I just kept driving it. Three months later I finally decided to sell it and it immediately stopped making the noise it had been making. Isn't that interesting?

Gary said, "I'll put an ad in the Trade Express for you."
He put in an ad that said, "Car for sale. Eclipse and the year, looks good, $6,500."
When he told me that, I said, "You didn't say it was beautiful and well taken care of, with great paint."

He didn't put any of those things in the ad. And it wasn't in the section with the other sports cars. They made a mistake and put in the Mercedes section.

Gary thought it was pretty funny because when I got the *Trade Express*, I said, "My car isn't in here."

He said, "Yes it is. I paid for the ad."
I said, "It's not in there."
The phone rang, and the person said, "I saw your car in the Trade Express."
Gary asked, "Where?"
The kid said, "In the Mercedes section."
Gary asked, "Why were you looking in the Mercedes section?"
He said, "I don't know. I was just flipping through the book. I knew there was something in here that I'd like."

Only two people called on it. The first one called and never showed up to look at it. The other was a seventeen-year-old kid who was totally excited: "Yeah, what does it have on it? And how many miles? And how much do you want for it? Please don't sell it. I'll be there tonight, I promise."

I said, "Okay, no problem. I'll wait for you." The car pulled in this kid.

Before I sold it to him, I said, "It may have a transmission problem. I'm not sure anymore."

He had it checked out by his mechanic. It came back with a clean bill of health. The mechanic said, "There's no transmission problem with this thing. This car is perfect. You are stupid if you don't buy this car."

It only had a transmission problem with me. It was saying, "I'm out of your life. You need something else. Time to move up a little." It definitely gave me the awareness of how to shift and change.

The car wanted to be with that kid. He started it up and the car sounded better than I'd ever heard it. I thought, "It's purring! Is it possible the car is happy?"

Apparently so. The car was happy and so was the kid.

His mom called me and said, "I just want to thank you so much. You have taught my son such a valuable lesson by the way you were forthright and honest."

His dad sent me an email saying, "We've been through a long car-buying process. I want to thank you because my son learned that it's possible to be honest and get what you want."

Wow. Cool car, eh?

Chapter Eleven

Manifesting Things

Humans have an agreement in this universe to create by linear constructs. A linear construct is: You have to do this to get that. It's the idea of linear source. It's a cause and effect viewpoint of creation that uses force and effort. Linear constructs tell us that time and money are real, and that there is a limited amount of energy in this universe. Most people, and certainly all humans, function from linear constructs. Mathematicians and scientists are, generally speaking, not human, so instead of saying, Okay, this is the way it is, they look to see what is possible. This is what we are encouraging you to do, as well.

GARY M. DOUGLAS & DR. DAIN HEER

De-Molecular Manifestation

Humanoids have the ability to de-molecularly manifest things into existence. What does this mean? It means you talk to the molecules, and the molecules change their structure and become what you ask for. We call this de-molecular manifestation. You ask the molecules to change their structure. They de-molecularize as they are and reconfigure themselves to become what you ask.

Molecular De-Manifestation

Molecular de-manifestation is where you ask something to go away. It works the same way. De-molecular manifestation and molecular de-manifestation are about your willingness to commune with everything; you ask the molecules to respond to your request—and they do.

Some people are resistant to doing this. They're not willing to ask and receive. But this is something you can learn to do. You can ask molecules to create what you wish.

Where Did All The Art Deco Pieces Come From?

Twenty years ago, when I (Gary) was really into antiques, I'd go into an antique shop and there would be a bunch of art deco pieces for sale. Twenty years later, after all the collectors in the world bought up all art deco pieces that were for sale, there are even more art deco pieces around than before. You have to ask: Is that physically possible—or are we creating something that's showing up?

Gosh, If I'd Seen That,
I Would Have Bought It

Have you ever walked into a store and found just the item you wanted, in your size, just exactly the way you wanted it, and the salesperson said, "Gosh, if I had seen that I would have bought it." Was it in the store before you got there—or did you actually create it? Did you de-molecularly manifest it, so it showed up? When that happened, did you think, *Wow, this is so serendipitous!*, or did you acknowledge that you created it?

A Medium Top And A Small Bottom

A friend told us that her dad was going to buy her an outfit. She usually wears a medium top and a small bottom, but she didn't tell him that. When he asked her what size she wore, she said, "Oh, a three or a four." So, he got her an outfit, and when she opened the package, there was a medium top and a small bottom.

How many times do these so-called little serendipitous events occur in your life—and how often do you acknowledge them for what they are? Something you have created.

I'd Like It To Perform Like An Audi

A lady who was attending one of our two-day Magic Seminars said she wanted a new car. She said, "Okay, this is the kind of car I'd like to create: I'd like it to be a 2001 or 2002 and have a great, solid engine. I'd like it to be fun and I'd like it to perform like an Audi."

We all went out to lunch together and in the parking lot of the restaurant was a red Audi convertible with a 'for sale' sign in the window. Ask and you shall receive. She called and it turned out the owner had lent the car to a friend to drive because he didn't have his car. The owner thought maybe her friend would drive it around and it would be seen by somebody who would like to buy it. She was asking $2,000 less than Blue Book value. The license plate on the car was *TIS ME*.

Is that enough magic for you?

Initially our friend couldn't receive it. She decided there had to be something wrong with it. She wouldn't buy the car because it came too easily. If it ain't hard, I ain't going to go for it. But by the second day of the class she had changed her point of view; she called the owner, made an offer and it was accepted.

Some people don't want to know they can create in this way. They have to give up their self-doubt and have faith in themselves. If they did, they would acknowledge that they can create the things they would like to have.

This is where the magic begins. If you're willing to ask the molecular structure of the universe to facilitate you, if you're willing to perceive what is possible instead of functioning from the linear construct of this reality, and if you're willing to trust yourself, then you can have a choice. Are you willing to give up the *I have no choice but . . .* point of view and claim and own your capacity to choose magic? Or do you want to hold on to your limitations?

Chapter Twelve

Performance Magic: Directing And Using Energy

We often coach singers and other performers on how to use energy to enhance their performance and connect with the audience in such a way that they become unforgettable. One of the things we like to do in our workshops is play with people's energy, their musical talents and abilities.

The same principles of performance apply whether you're pitching a song or you're pitching a job. It doesn't matter whether you are singing a tune, teaching a class, conducting a meeting, interviewing for a job or trying to get your product or service into the hands of people who want it. Getting the result you desire has to do with the way you connect with your public; it has to do with the way you direct and use energy.

When you perform, you want the audience to feel connected to you. Before you walk onstage, begin to pull massive amounts of energy from everybody in the audience through every pore in your body and your being. As you walk onstage, continue to do this until you know everyone is connected to you. You will feel your heart open up a little bit. Then, as you perform, continue to pull energy and let an equal flow go back to the audience. After the performance, keep pulling energy and let a little trickle go back to the audience so they can't get you off their minds.

There's the pre-performance pull, the equalization of the flow during the performance, and the after-performance trickle that goes back to the audience. The pull attracts them initially, and when you keep pulling the energy from them, they experience a pull in your direction and connect with you. When you let a little trickle go back to them at the end, it lets them know you're the source.

Because you're an infinite being, you can do this for billions of people at the same time. Most people tend to finish a performance or finish a presentation and shut their energy off. This is a mistake. Never ever shut your energy off, because when you do, you are breaking the connection people feel with you. Suddenly you're out of their lives. This also applies to creating a relationship. If you're in relationship with somebody, never break the connection. Recognize you have infinite possibilities and capacities. You can maintain connections to billions of people at the same time. This is the way you sell your records or your books or your products.

Get The Feeling Of What It's Like
To Perform In Front Of Ten People

In our workshops, before we have people go up on stage to perform in front of all of us, we ask them to get the feeling of what it's like to perform in front of ten people. They do this, and then we tell them to revoke, recant, rescind, reclaim, renounce, destroy and uncreate all the feelings and reactions that came up around that.

Then we ask them to get the feeling of performing in front of fifty people. Then one hundred people. Then two hundred fifty people, each time destroying and uncreating the feelings that came up. Then we go to five hundred people. Some people get scared and can't get past the idea of performing in front of five hundred people. That's the maximum number of people they'll allow into their lives. Then we ask them to get the feeling of what it's like to perform in front of one thousand people, destroying and un-creating the feelings that come up. Then five thousand people, ten thousand people, fifty thousand people, one hundred thousand people. What is the feeling of performing in front of one hundred thousand people? Destroy and uncreate that feeling.

Then we go to five hundred thousand people. A million people. Five million. What are the feelings that come up around performing in front of five million people? Can you destroy and uncreate all of those? And now ten million people. Destroy and uncreate everything that doesn't allow you to perform in front of ten million people. Now you're going to be performing for a billion people around the world on TV and everybody's watching you.

All of the lifetimes in which you got pulled off the stage, and all the things you're not willing to receive, the rotten tomatoes and raw eggs, the gong, and everything else you decided you can't receive, would you destroy and uncreate all of those?

Everything that does not allow you to remember all the lifetimes in which you were the greatest performer that ever was, and all the decisions you made about fame and fortune and how hideous it was to be seen all the time and never have a moment of privacy, can you destroy and uncreate all of those?

We ask people, "What is the one thing you're unwilling to receive from your performance besides total adulation, total love and everybody wanting to have sex with you?", and we get some interesting answers. Some people say, "Criticism," others say, "Success." What's your answer? What's the one thing you're unwilling to receive from your performance besides total adulation, total love and everybody wanting to have sex with you?

You have to be willing to receive anything from your audience.

We did these processes with a lady in one of our classes, and when we saw her ten months later, she told us she had gotten a CD together, performed as a featured singer at the Mustang Lounge, and had been having her singles played on the radio, which is unheard of in today's music business.

> I asked her, "How are your pre-performance jitters now?"
> She said, "I haven't had any since we did those processes. The pre-performance butterflies are gone. They don't exist. I walk out on the stage and I instantly sing great. I never think I'm not going to."

When you're willing to receive anything, all the limitations, the butterflies, the jitters and worries go away, and you can be present as you, singing your heart out and receiving whatever people are willing to give you.

Are You Willing To Stop Every Conversation In The Room?

If you're going to be a great performer (or a great public speaker, teacher or leader), you have to be willing to stop every conversation in the room and make it impossible for anybody to have a conversation once you start to perform. It's not the volume or the force of your performance that creates this result; it's your willingness to pull everybody into your universe.

Without exception, this is what great performers do. Singers as diverse as Dolly Parton, Luciano Pavarotti, David Bowie, and Bob Dylan suck everybody into their universe when they perform. They're willing to have sex with everybody in the whole place. They're willing to bring everybody to orgasm with their voice.

Pull The Sexualness Of The Universe Into Your Body

When you sing something slow and seductive, pull everybody into it so that you've got them having sex with you while you're singing, not by the gyrations of your body, but by the energy you create. Pull all the sexualness in the universe into your body and sing sex. Sexualness is the healing energy, the nurturing energy, the caring energy, the creative energy, the joyful energy and the expansive energy of the universe. That's what you sing to people. You're singing to the orgasmic quality in each and every person. You put the promise of copulation into your song without ever doing it.

Bringing sexualness, or the expansive energy of the universe, into a song is so powerful it can create big changes in a person's voice. When we coach people to do this, it changes elements in their throats that don't permit them to get full range. So, not only will performers' ability to pull people into their universes improve, but their voices will change, as well. People have told us it's actually like having sex on stage. They experience a different cellular expression in their bodies. And when you're having sex on stage, everybody in the audience thinks they're having sex with you. That's what performers like Madonna do. She makes you think you're having sex with her while she's performing. We try to facilitate that for everyone who sings with us, so they have an opportunity to create that result in every person that they communicate with.

We have a friend in Nashville who is an awesome songwriter. The first time he presented one of his songs, he sang it on the demo tape and the guy listening to it said, "Who's that singing? It's a pretty good song, but he's got a terrible voice! You need somebody with a better voice to demo it." Well, our friend got his friend, Garth Brooks, to record the song, and they bought it. But it was interesting: He was a great musician, he wrote the best songs, but he had the worst fucking voice I (Gary) have ever heard in my life.

One day when he was in the Access Level II Class, I asked him if he'd like to try some things with his voice. We took the energy in his throat where he couldn't sing and we opened it up. We worked at it for twenty or thirty minutes at the most, because that's about all anybody can take, and I said, "Okay, don't sing anything else tonight. Wait until tomorrow. Bring your guitar and sing."

The next day in class when he started to sing, his wife burst into tears, I burst into tears, and everyone in the class had goose bumps. It was a totally different voice. Since then, he has been Center Stage at the Grand Ole Opry, he's put out an album with some other guys that's sold fifty thousand copies, and he's taken tours around Ireland, England and the United States, singing his songs. And people are saying things to him like, "Hey, your voice sounds pretty good. What are you doing? It's getting better all the time."

The More She Sang, The Louder They Talked

After a recent workshop, a group of us went to a restaurant where a singer was performing. Everybody in the place was talking while she sang. The more she sang, the louder everyone talked. They weren't going to listen. What was happening here? The performer wasn't willing to cut the crowd's conversations with the sexualness that she could have put out there. She wasn't willing to promise that they could get something better than their conversations, better than sex and better than going home alone.

This particular lady walked by us on her way to the bathroom. I (Gary) looked up at her and smiled, but she couldn't have it. She put up barriers. I said, "Wow, isn't that interesting? I just smiled. I was saying, 'Hi, how are you?' but she wasn't willing to look at me."

She was not willing to have all conversation stop at the sound of her voice. She was not willing to be seen and perceived, and she was not willing to be received. If you're going to do a performance, if you're going to do any sort of public speaking or teaching, you have to be willing to be seen. She wasn't willing to let us be in her universe; she wasn't willing to invite us into her universe and make us think she was the best thing that ever happened.

An Exercise You Can Do

If you'd like to improve your ability to be seen and perceived, here is an exercise you can do: Go to a coffee shop. Walk in the door, stand to one side and pull energy from everybody in the room until they turn around and look at you. Then you can walk out. Or you can stay and buy something if you want to. But pull energy from everyone in the place until they turn around and look at you. To do that, you have to be willing to truly be seen and to receive whatever anybody might send toward you.

When Gary asked me (Dain) to do this, I thought, Okay, I'm going to make this happen. I used effort to pull the energy. That didn't work. No one turned around. Then I just asked the energy to pull, and people started turning around to look at me. At first they seemed kind of surprised, like *What am I looking over here for? There must be something important over here. What is it?* It was me, pulling energy. I was the most important thing to them right then.

At first I wasn't willing to be seen. I put up barriers, like the singer did with Gary, but as I practiced it more, I became willing to have people look at me and to just be there with them.

Are You Willing To Receive Being Mobbed?

Are you willing to perform and to receive people throwing flowers and money at you? Are you willing to receive massive amounts of money, gold, the crown jewels and people giving up their titles for you? You have to be willing to receive being mobbed. You have to be willing to receive being stalked. Notice that we're not saying you have to be mobbed or that you have to be stalked. We're saying you have to be willing to receive being mobbed, because when you are truly willing to receive being mobbed, you are also willing to know when that's going to happen so you can be some place else before the mob gets there. And if it happens and you don't get away fast enough, there's something else you can do. You can make yourself infinite—bigger than the universe—and nobody will notice you're there. You can stand in the middle of the crowd and nobody will see you.

Gary often does this. If Gary and I (Dain) go out to dinner and I think the waitress is cute, Gary will make himself infinite and the waitress will sit down and talk to me as though he's not even there. I'll be thinking, *Thanks, Gary, you're a good friend.* It's amazing to see him do this. He'll be right behind me and people will not see him. You can do that, as well. If you make yourself infinite, bigger than the universe, nobody will know you're there.

But you definitely do not want to make yourself infinite when you're on stage. When you're on stage, you want to pull energy from everyone in the place. Some people have judgments or misunderstandings about this. They're not willing to pull massive amounts of energy through their bodies. You need to be able to pull the chrome off a '58 Buick that's still in 1958.

You should be willing to receive the energy as though it would push you over, but it won't knock you down. In reality, it's pulling *through* you. Some people think there's so-called bad or negative energy or that energy contains intentions or other evil stuff that can harm them as they pull it through themselves. Have you made judgments to do with that crock of shit? There's just energy. It's neither good nor bad, right nor wrong. It's only our judgments that can make anything good or bad. Will you destroy and uncreate all those considerations, please?

For some people who have strong psychic abilities, it can be a little different, because they pick up every thought, feeling and emotion within a hundred and fifty thousand miles of themselves.

When they pull energy, they can also pick up on all the thoughts, feelings and emotions of others around them. That's a talent and ability they have. Even if you're less psychic, you can do that, too, if you choose to, but you don't want to do that. What you want is to create an energy connection and the way you can do it is to pull energy from everybody in the room until you feel your heart start to open up a little bit.

How Do You Energize The Audience?

We've discovered that the more somebody pulls energy from you, the more energized you feel. Think about a truly great performance you've seen. Didn't you feel unbelievably energized by it? Is that the ultimate control of a performance? Great performers energize the audience by pulling energy from them. Try it. As you get energized, guess how much more energy your audience will give you. Guess how much better your performance is going to get. Guess how much more energized the audience will become.

Are You Willing To Give Everybody In The Audience An Orgasm?

We can take this even a step further. There are particular parts of a person's body that you can touch into energetically to create an orgasm in their body. As a performer, you should be willing to give everybody in the audience an orgasm. Are you willing to do this? If not, everything you've done to stop yourself from perceiving, knowing, being and receiving how to give everybody in the audience an orgasm just by hitting the right note, the right tone, the right vibration, the right energy...will you destroy and uncreate all that and claim and own the talent and ability to do it?

Pulling energy also works when you're being photographed. When I (Gary) have my picture taken, I always pull the entirety of the energy of the universe through me. In New York, a tiny little photo of me was used in a small publication in an ad for an expo. It was one inch by one inch, all grainy. I was standing in front of some people who were looking at the ad and they said, "Oh, let's go to that one. That one looks like a good lecture." They looked at me as they walked by and didn't realize I was the guy in the picture. The energy of the picture pulled them in. Whenever you have a photograph taken, pull energy in from all over the universe through you and everybody will fall into your picture. That's the magic.

When You Pull Energy, You Create
A Connection With The Audience

You feel a much stronger connection to performers who pull energy from you. They're the ones you want to see. You feel like they're closer to you, like there is less distance between you, less of a separation. That's an important effect that gets created. When you perform and you pull energy, you create a connection with the audience.

How do you do it? You pull energy until you feel your heart open, and then you equalize the flow. You just ask the energy to pull. You don't have to do anything. You don't even have to look at anybody. You can put all your attention on one person. And then, at the end of your performance, you don't turn off your energy. You let a little trickle go back to your audience until you feel your heart open even more. That sets it up so that they will never ever be able to forget you. That's how you create your future audience. This also works with someone you're attracted to. They will talk about you. They will wonder about you. They'll ask questions about you.

Are You Willing To Be A
Nine-Point Earthquake?

Sometimes in our workshops we ask performers to pull energy and to look at the person in the audience they would be least likely to have sex with. Or three or four of them. We tell them to sing so that they turn those people on. We say, "Okay, we want you to make those people so happy they will want to go home with you."

Are you willing to be a nine-point earthquake in people's lives? Look at every single person in the audience and let each one of them know that they're the one you want to go home with. Do this when you first come out on the stage. Start to suck everyone into your universe when you first start strumming your guitar. Some people use a band as a way of covering themselves up. They don't show up. But you want to be the point everyone is looking at. Everybody is thinking about you. Everybody's wanting to take you home. Now we're talking.

We had one of our workshop participants do this. In the audience there were three glum women who were so near death as to almost not be available. He began to sing and within the first three lines of his song, the first one smiled. Within another three lines, the second one smiled, and within ten lines, the third one smiled. They continued to smile, and at the end of the song, they clapped longer and harder than anyone else.

People can't see what they give to others. Why won't you see what you give? It's not about effort. You have to take the effort out of it. If you learn to direct energy, you'll have people falling at your feet as you walk by.

Do You Want A Job?

If you want to get a job, you do the same thing. Before you get there, start to pull energy from the people who will interview you. When you walk into the office, equalize the flow. When you leave, keep pulling and let a little trickle go back. When you do this, they will have a hard time forgetting you. They will not know what it is about you but they'll say *There's something about that guy*, and you'll get hired every time. But you better want the job or you're going to be in trouble.

This doesn't just apply to performers or employment. It applies any time you desire to create a connection. Do this any time you desire people to not be able to get you off their minds, whether it's a job or a person you'd like to create a connection with.

It Doesn't Require Effort

It's important to remember that it's soft. It doesn't require a lot of effort. You just ask the energy to pull. *I'll pull now, create a little flow back, okay, cool.* It's that easy, and you just allow it to continue. You don't have to work at it. You just ask it to happen and then the universe says, *Oh, ask and you shall receive. Okay, cool.* It's that easy.

The person doesn't even have to be in the same room. They can be across the world and the effect still occurs. That's what creates the place of more desire for your song or your product.

We tend to think that our product is something tangible. We think that what we give to others is a *thing*. No, it's the *energy*. What you're creating when you're performing, in particular, is a level of energy that invites people into a different possibility.

When you're creating art or literature, when you're creating anything, you have to realize that the value of you is what you create. It's the energy you create, not the thing you give somebody.

Sexualness Is Receiving And Gifting

Sexualness is receiving, which is why we're stressing it. Unless you're willing to receive everything, you have nothing to give. There's no gift unless you can receive. You have to be able to receive in order to gift. You have to gift in order to receive. It's all simultaneous. The beauty of this is that when you perform in this way, you are simultaneously giving and receiving—and so is your audience.

When you add sexualness—the healing, the nurturing, the caring, the expansiveness, the creativity, the infinite possibilities and the joyful expression of life to what you are doing, when you bring that into your being—you change everybody around you. You bring those possibilities into their universe as well as your own. You show them that those things can actually be in their lives.

You have the ability to create that sense of possibility in somebody's life, whether it's by singing or public speaking, or through a conversation. By embodying those qualities, you take down barriers and present a new possibility to others. You're saying, *Look, you can be this, too.*

Chapter Thirteen

Lyrics

Sometimes singers do not understand their lyrics, and sometimes they have to create the emotions being expressed in the songs they sing. We coached a woman who was singing "Stormy Weather." She was saying it's stormy weather because she lost her man, but she didn't mean it. Maybe she was thinking, *I finally got rid of that son of a bitch*, and now I'm happy. It wasn't real to her that it was stormy weather because she and her man weren't together. Maybe for her, it was sunny weather.

A different song that was more in line with what was real to her might have been a better choice. But, really, do performers sing lyrics because they're real to them, or do they perform lyrics for people who have those lines as their point of view?

We asked her to go out fifty miles in all directions and see all the people who were longing for their loved one and missing their man or their woman and saying, *Oh, poor me.* We asked her to bring that energy into her body, and when she did so, to notice where her throat clamped down. Then, we asked her to sing from that place, to create the emotion of the song. There's a clamp in the throat, and people who are in that emotion function from that place. It's where they speak from when they say, *"I'm missing my man. What am I going to do without my lover? I'm going to die."*

She did that. She picked up the energy of the song and when she started to sing again, her voice quavered with the emotion, and it was so moving that people in the audience started to cry.

Here's something you can do as an example, right now: Go out one hundred miles in all directions and feel all the homeless people in the world and think about being a homeless person. Feel the energy of that. Pull that energy into your body. What closes down on you? If you were going to play the part of a homeless person or if you were going to sing as a homeless person, you would have to be able to pull that energy into your body and find a place you could speak or sing it from. You would have to deliver the words and the energy from that place, because that's the truth of being there. That's what creates a great performance, as opposed to a good one.

When we've done this exercise in our workshops, we hear qualities come into people's voices that we didn't hear before. Pulling that energy in creates a vibrato and suddenly the emotion is there. It's a way of embodying the energy of the lyrics. What comes out of performers' mouths is the emotion those people live. This also works for actors and actresses.

I (Gary) worked with an actress who was going to play a queen. She said, "I'm just not able to cut it with this part."

I said, "Go out five thousand miles in all directions to all the queens in the world and all the places they were not allowed to talk." She did that, and what came out of her mouth was completely different from before. She lost her old self and became the queen.

Chapter Fourteen

Magic, Work And Money

Creation Is The Fun Part: Money Is A By-Product

One of the very interesting differences between humans and humanoids is that humanoids don't work for money. When a humanoid creates something or performs a service and someone else receives it and is grateful for it, that's it. That's the end of the exchange. They say, *That's cool!* and they're done. Their energy is complete on it.

Money has nothing to do with a humanoid's creative capacity or what motivates them. The money is a by-product. It's a secondary result. Most humanoids would prefer not to deal with money, and not to put attention on it because it has nothing to do with their creative capacity. For them, creation is the fun part. When they create something, they look around and ask *What else can I create?* Creation is what moves the energy for them. All the energy in a humanoid universe goes into creation.

If you're a humanoid, it's important to be aware of this, because unless you are willing to receive the byproduct of your work or service, you're not going to get paid for your efforts. You're actually going to push it away. You're going to stop money from coming in. You're going to refuse to collect it even though it's due to you. You won't ask for it.

Asking Is Different From Receiving

You have to be willing to ask for the money. You have to ask—and you shall receive. Asking is actually different from receiving. They're two different things. You think *If it falls out of the sky, sure, I'll take it, but I'm not sure I'm willing to ask for it.* But you have to be able to ask for money with ease.

Humanoids can get confused because they can't do things for money, yet the point of view they grew up with was *You only do things for money and if you don't get paid for it, it's not worth doing.* But it never works out for humanoids when they try to work for money. They try to fit into the human reality of money, and this causes them great difficulty. It's important to understand that as humanoids, we have a different view, and we also have to be willing to receive the by-product of our endeavors. We have to be able to ask for—and receive—the money.

Are You Willing To Receive A Gift?

Do you realize that when some people give you money, it is a gift? Most of us think of it as a payment or an obligation, and many times we disavow and destroy the gift. We are not willing to receive gifts that others give us; we're not willing to have the money, the sex, the love, whatever it is. You won't receive love from the man you're with for what reason? You won't receive money from your client or your customer for what reason?

Some people think that if they receive, then it involves responsibility and other entanglements. They've decided it's easier not to receive. Excuse me, do you have the point of view that money is an obligation and a responsibility, and you've got to use it right and you've got to handle it right, and if you don't handle it right, you're going to die in poverty? That's a good one.

But . . .

Sometimes people tell us they can accept gifts from others easily enough, but they have trouble accepting money. They say things like, *I can accept gifts, but I have trouble accepting money.* But. Listen for the *but*. People use *but* to counter what they've just said. They make it nonexistent.

That *but* cuts out the magic; it does away with the magical possibilities. *I can receive but . . .* Once you say *but*, you're negating everything you said about being able to receive. You discount and destroy everything that came before it. You're saying, *I really can't have the magic.* You're trying to solidify what you have decided you will receive, as opposed to what you won't receive.

Don't be a but-head.

You Are A Gift

Not only do you have to be willing to receive love and money and whatever else people want to give you, you also have to be willing to receive you. If you're refusing to be who you truly are, you're asking to be underpaid. You are devaluing you. When you're unwilling to be you, when you're unwilling to be as dynamic and fabulous and amazing, the gift that you truly are, then you devalue you.

Are you trying to prove that not being you is correct? That means that you will never let yourself have all the money you could have. You won't let yourself have all the joy that you could have. You won't let yourself have all the freedom you could have. And you won't let yourself have all the consciousness you could have. All of this, because you're always trying to prove that there's a reason for your devaluation. For you not being you.

You must be willing to see the value of you. Are you discounting your capacity, your ability, your talents, your value, and the gift that you are? What would it take for you to claim, own or acknowledge and actually be able to receive the gift that you are? You are a gift because you are a humanoid. You are a gift because you are creative. You are a gift because you are conscious. You are gift because you are aware.

Chapter Fifteen

There's Magic In That 10 Percent

We often coach people on money issues, and one of the things they tell us is they don't save money. When money shows up in their lives, instead of saving it, they spend it.

There is something you need to know about money: You need to put away 10 percent of what you earn. Put away 10 percent of every dollar that comes in and don't spend it on anything, ever. When we tell people this, they often act as if they've heard the most insane advice. But putting away 10 percent is the single-most dynamic thing you can do to increase your money flows.

Over and over again, people tell us it works. If you put away 10 percent of every dollar that comes in, within a year your whole financial condition will have changed. Some people say it changes within a few months.

Why Does It Work?

Why does it work? It works because for you as a humanoid, energy is the source of everything. The energy of having that money set aside creates the willingness to receive more. You start to request more of the world. When I (Gary) had saved a certain amount, I went, *Whoa, that's cool. I wonder what it would take to have twice this amount in the bank.* And money started to pour in. I went, *Well, this is cool. How does it get any better than this?* And more money came in. I said, *This is really cool. How do I get more than this?*

Putting money aside and letting it grow takes money out of the place where it's significant. It no longer has to do with bare survival. Having a growing amount of cash puts you into a place where you realize you can actually create it and have it. The thing that stops us from having and creating money is the idea we don't have enough. There is magic in that little 10 percent. When your savings gets to a certain amount you suddenly feel secure. All those safety issues you've always had, all those ideas that there's never going to be enough, vanish. You become more and more abundant. You can even keep your money at home, lay it out on the bed and roll naked in it.

It's important to understand why you are putting away your 10 percent. We returned to New Zealand a year after we had done a seminar there, and a guy who had been in the class said, "That shit you're talking about, the 10 percent, doesn't work."

I (Gary) asked him, "Have you been doing it?"

He said, "Yeah."

I said, "Okay, tell me about it."

He said, "Well, I've been doing it ever since you told me I had to and . . ."

Hmm. He was doing it because I told him he had to save 10 percent? Does that sound like he was honoring himself? Does that sound like there was any joy or any acknowledgment of his ability to put 10 percent away because he was so friggin' abundant, that it wasn't going to matter? Does this sound like he was focused on bringing more abundance into his life? No. He didn't have that point of view. He did it because I told him he had to do it—which isn't what I told him at all.

Can I Use My 10 Percent To Pay Off Debts?

People ask us if they can use their 10 percent to pay off their debts. The answer is no. The way to create *additional* money to pay off your debt is by putting 10 percent away. That's how you increase the amount of money you take in. Which is more valuable, you or your debt? If you pay your debts before you set aside your 10 percent, you're making your debts more important. Do you make sure to pay all your bills on time? Have you ever noticed that you get more and more bills? It's because you're telling the universe, I like to pay my bills. You're honoring your bills above you, so the universe gives you more bills to pay. Isn't that cool?

The value of the 10 percent is that you're honoring yourself first. You get the money and you put it away before anything happens. You're telling the universe—and you're telling yourself—that you honor you. You honor you more than your bills. If it means you've got to play catch up on your bills, then do that. Honor yourself.

This busts you out of the idea you've been functioning from, that bills are supreme: *Bills are the important thing—I've got to pay my bills.* Instead you're saying, *I'm honoring me. I'm more valuable than these bills.* Can you imagine you being even more valuable than bills? What would that do for your financial situation?

Don't Spend It!

Setting 10 percent aside is about *having* money, it's not about spending it. Occasionally you might do something silly, like decide you have so much that can spend it. I (Dain) had a nice amount saved, and I decided, I'm going to go into my savings to pay for a few things.

I went into the 10 percent and spent a large part of it, and instantly people stopped calling me for sessions. Everything dried up. I could feel it happening. I felt like I was walking in a desert all alone. Nobody wanted to have anything to do with me. It took me a few weeks to realize I'd spent my 10 percent and I said, *You know what? From now on, no matter what it takes, no matter what happens, I'm going to put 10 percent away.* I've done it ever since and as I continue to put it away my income keeps increasing.

What you're saying when you spend your 10 percent is, *I have no choice but to spend this money.* No choice is what? Have you taken away your infiniteness? Instead ask, *Okay, what's it going to take for me to create enough money? Okay, what else do I have to do? What else is possible?* Have you made your reality about no choice rather than *infinite choice?* Will you destroy and uncreate everything you've done to create that, please? The real magic in life is the willingness to have infinite choice.

You've got to change your perspective. You're living from I can't, rather than I can. You're living from I don't have, rather than I have. You've got to change your point of view—that's what is locking you up right now. And the way you change your point of view is by saving 10 percent.

When you have money in the bank and you're saving that 10 percent all the time, you might get to a certain point where you think about buying an item. You might think, *Okay, I've got the money. Now, do I truly want to buy this thing? I could take the money out of the bank and buy it. But do I really want it?* Suddenly you'll find you don't desire it any more because it's not something you can't have. It's something you can have. Our desire to purchase things is often based on what we think we can't have.

One time I (Gary) said to somebody, "I can't wait until the day I have one hundred thousand dollars in my checking account at all times."

> He said, "That would be interest bearing, right?"
> I said, "No."
> He said, "You wouldn't put it into an interest-bearing account?"
> I said, "No."
> He asked, "Why wouldn't you do that?"
> I said, "Because if I had that much money I wouldn't care about that piddly amount of interest." When are you going to let yourself have so much money that you're not concerned about the pennies?

Can I Put My 10 Percent Into Investments?

It doesn't matter if you put your 10 percent under your pillow or into a savings account. Just set it aside. Your 10 percent doesn't get invested. You don't put it into investments. But if you're going to invest in anything, invest in something that you totally know is going to work and something that you energetically recognize is the right vibration for you. It doesn't matter what anybody else suggests. Don't give your power to somebody who says, "This is good stock. It's going to go up." I (Gary) tried that, and it all went down. I said, *Okay, from now on, unless it feels right for me, I'm not going to do it.* So, I've invested in a few stocks where I said, *Okay, this one feels right, I'll do this.* And all of them have gone up.

Of course, when I decided it was time to sell them, I didn't do it—and they all went down, because I didn't follow my knowing; I listened to my stockbroker rather than myself. Mistake.

Stop Pretending You've Got To Take Care Of The Kids

A parent asked us about what to tell her kids after she put the 10 percent away and there was nothing left over to buy things the kids were asking for. She didn't like the feeling she was creating energetically when she said, "No, we can't buy that," or "No, we don't have the money for that."

We told her to tell the kids, "I don't have the money for that right now. Would you guys like to do something to earn part of it and I'll help you with it?"

Stop pretending that you've got to take care of the kids. Kids are incredible. They can take care of themselves. Your kids have more power in their little fingers than most people have in their whole bodies. Teach them about living in the question. What happens when they ask, *Okay, I wonder what it would take for this to happen?* They'll create some kind of magic that will knock your socks off. They'll go out and open a roadside stand selling lemonade and everybody will stop.

I (Gary) see little kids doing the roadside thing all the time and if I see Mom hanging out there with them, helping them with it I don't stop. But when I see kids putting themselves out there and going, *Hi, come on in,* and creating the energy of it, I stop every time and give them a dollar for a twenty-five-cent drink. Why do I do that? I want to validate them for the energy they're putting out. I want them to get that what they're creating is worth more than they're asking. What would happen if we did that sort of thing all the time?

Chapter Sixteen

Do You Have To Love A Product In Order To Sell It?

Many humanoids who work in sales believe they have to love a product in order to sell it. They think they have to believe in the integrity of the product. They say, I can only sell a good product. This sounds great until you realize they're basing their ability to sell on a judgment: Is the product good or is the product bad? They think it's bad to sell a product when they don't believe in it. The problem here is their judgment makes them blind to the buyer. Do they know what the buyer wants? No. Have they asked the buyer whether the product is needed and wanted? No.

People get confused about this and the reason they get confused is that they have a fixed idea. They think they have it right when they sell a product that is good. But to whatever degree you think you have the right point of view, you have a limitation you cannot overcome.

A friend who is a salesperson told me, "I'm really successful when I ask the universe, *Who is looking for this product?*"

Another friend who is in sales told me there are some things she'd rather sell because she thinks they're cooler than other things, but she has come to understand that's a judgment, and she doesn't really know what a buyer wants. When someone goes to her and they want a particular thing, what immediately comes to her mind is the item she thinks is the best. When her buyer picks out something else, she thinks, *Oh no, you don't like that.* But then she remembers she has to allow them to have their own point of view and decision.

A lot of times, salespeople are way more familiar with a product than the buyer, and they make judgments about what's best for the other person. They decide what the buyer should have. They think they have a responsibility to choose for the buyer, but they're mistaken.

When buyers decide something is perfect for them, or when they make the judgment that there is no other product as good as the one they've chosen, it doesn't matter how much of a better deal you give them or how great the other product is, they will never see it. They cut off every perception in the world with every decision and every judgment they make.

What does this mean to you as someone working in sales? It means you have to be in communion with your buyer. You have to honor what they desire.

Do You Try To Give The Best Service You Possibly Can?

The same principle applies in providing a service. Do you try to give the best service you possibly can? Do you do your best all the time? Do you always give full value—and more? This is another one of those things that sounds great—but are you paying attention to what your client or your customer wants? If your efforts to do the best you can have made you blind to what people want from you, you're not providing great service.

I (Dain) started practicing Access when I was a chiropractor. I was doing chiropractic and my practice evolved into an unusual sort of bodywork and energy work that provided a lot of change for people who were willing to receive it. When I first started out, I tried to shove as much energy as I could through a person's body to prove I was actually doing something for them. I wanted to show them the value of my services. I felt I had to justify the money I was charging and show them that something had happened.

A lot of us have done this. We try to justify what we're charging for our services by trying much too hard. I'd give as much as I could in every session. It didn't matter if people could only receive a five, I'd still give them one hundred twenty.

Who had to take on the burden of what they weren't willing to receive? I did, and my body did. I would do one session and I'd have to take a nap so my body could rejuvenate. I finally realized that few people are willing to receive the infinite possibilities that are available. Few people are willing to receive the amount that I can give if I'm on 100 percent.

I was shutting off my own perception about how much people could receive, and I was giving way more than they were willing to have. As my style of working with people evolved, my understanding of how to use energy increased. I finally realized that if someone can only receive 5 percent of what I can give, and if I give them 6 percent, I am not honoring them. I'm actually dishonoring who they are, what they are and what they're asking of me. I'm trying to shove more into their universe than they are capable of receiving. In giving them 100 percent when they could only receive five, I was not only harming my body, but I was taking them to a place where they weren't comfortable; I was shaking up their universe too much.

When I started giving them a five instead, the sessions got much easier and people would get off the table grateful for what I had done instead of saying, *What the hell hit me? I don't ever want to go through that again.* Giving them a five was also much easier on my body because it was exactly what they were asking of me.

Have you shut off your perceiving, knowing, being and receiving in order to prove to yourself that you're doing a good job? Do you give much more than is needed, rather than recognizing what another person can truly receive?

I (Gary) have worked with people where I knew I could take them to the moon and change their whole life in one hour, but all they wanted was to change their underwear. I finally understood that I had to let them change only as much as they were comfortable changing. That was all they could have. That's what they wanted.

I learned to charge the same amount of money for a session that produced small changes as I did for the person whose whole life was transformed by an hour's work.

You want to help, and you want to demonstrate what you can do, but you've got to stop trying to decide what's right for other people. The difference between knowing you can do it and proving you can do it is pretty big. When you give people what they can't receive, you're trying to prove to yourself that you can do it. You're not simply knowing you can do it.

You've got to get to the point where you're willing to know how good you truly are, and to understand that others can receive whatever they can receive. If you give them that, they will be grateful. Oftentimes they will pay you more money for what seems like less, which is really weird. You do significantly less than you're capable of, and they give you more money—because you've given them exactly what they wanted and needed.

It's not a matter of equating the amount of change someone got with the amount of money you receive. In this case, the money truly is the by-product. Does that make sense?

Other People's Choices

Everybody has choice; this is something about the universe you have to honor. If people choose to be homeless, that is their choice. You cannot change that for them without their participation. It's only when they decide they don't want to be homeless anymore that you can change something.

The same thing applies with what someone will receive. People come to us and they want to do little tiny baby steps in Access. They'll have a session once a month and they'll come to a class once a year and they don't want to go any faster than that. There are other people who come and they say, "I want to do Foundation, One, Two, Three, and everything else you've got. How soon can you do it? How soon can I get this and what's it going to take to do that? How can I get more, and why don't you write books? Why isn't there more stuff out there? What's the matter with you and why aren't you giving me more?" Those guys are few and far between. They take in everything you can possibly give. I (Gary) give to the exact degree somebody can receive because I've learned to do so over time. I used to be like Dain; I would try to prove to people that they could have everything.

I once had the experience of doing a session with somebody after teaching a class. Afterwards, we had a long conversation about what allowance is really about, and I thought, *This is so cool. He's really getting it!* But the next thing that came out of his mouth indicated that he hadn't taken in a single thing I thought I had given him that day. He heard what I said and then instantaneously went right back to his old way of functioning because he wasn't willing to give it up. I assumed that he was willing to give it up because he was willing to listen. But willingness to listen is not necessarily the point.

That's the reason it's important to ask a question. If you ask a question, you'll find out exactly what somebody's willing to receive from you. You'll find out exactly what they want to take from you. You'll find out exactly what is possible for them.

Do You Have Employees?

Do you have employees? They are also eager to demonstrate how much they can do. When I hire people to work for me, I always ask them what their job is. I never tell them what they've got to do. I always ask them what they're *going* to do, and I usually end up getting twenty times what I'm paying for. Why is that? Because they want to prove how good they are. This is not taking advantage of them. People are absolutely grateful to be able to provide everything they can provide.

Chapter Seventeen

Oneness And Gender Assignment

Oneness

The infinite Oneness that we truly have and are is the source for everything that we would consider to be magic. As oneness, we can perceive, know, be and receive all things without judgment. Oneness includes everything and judges nothing. In oneness, you are willing to receive everything on the planet; you are in communion with all things; you are total receiving, and there is no judgment. But as soon as you say, *I am this*, you create a limitation. This is what happens when you go into gender assignment.

Gender assignment is your definition of your sexual nature and role. It's always a judgment, and it always involves cutting off some aspect of you in order to make your designated gender assignment work. As soon as you say, *I'm a straight male*, you refer to a norm, which then becomes a source of division and separation. You cut off your ability to receive from everything else in the universe. That's it. You won't receive energy from plants, you won't receive energy from animals. And you especially won't receive energy from other men.

With gender assignment, instead of embracing the sexualness in everyone, we think, *It's not appropriate for me to see the sexual energy in my daughter or my same-sex friend or my mother or my brother, because that means I'm having bad thoughts.* No. I want to be able to appreciate my male friend's sexual energy as well as a woman's or a cat's or a tree's. You've got to be able to see the gift that each person is and receive it without judgment.

People sometimes misidentify what we're saying and think we're talking about copulation. Well, we don't copulate with cats, but we do receive their sexualness. It's important to recognize that because you can have the sexualness or sexual energy of someone, it doesn't mean you have to go to bed with them.

Oneness Has No Gender Assignment

Oneness has no gender assignment and it has no judgment about gender, whom you sleep with, or anything like that. When we go into gender assignment, as most of us on this planet do, we assign a certain set of characteristics to ourselves and we create limitations based on those characteristics.

We say, *I'm a woman; therefore I don't have big muscles. I can't lift things; therefore I must manipulate men to do things for me. I must be the effect of all men because I can't do things myself.* Or it's, *I'm a man. My brain's in my penis and therefore I am the effect of women. Whatever they want, I do.* Gender assignment means, I'm a woman. I have the babies. I'm a man. I provide the sperm for babies. Either way, there is separation and limitation, and no validation of the oneness we truly are.

We Simulate Who We Are Based On Gender

We simulate who we are based on gender. *I'm a female. I'm a woman. That means ____. I'm a male. I'm a man. That means ____.* Is that really who we are? No, of course not. Does buying into gender assignment create limitation? Yes, of course it does. It creates myriad limitations.

We buy into the limitations as though they are the truth of who we are, or we buy into the limitations and then we fight them to prove we're not really limited by them. With women's lib, for example, women fought the idea they were *just women.* They fought to show they were something greater. And men who fought the idea they were out just to get laid became SNAGs—Sensitive, New-Age Guys. None of that kind of resisting or fighting against gives you freedom.

With gender assignment, we are run by rules, definitions and judgments that keep us from choosing for ourselves and being at ease with the choices we make, because gender assignment has nothing to do with who we really are. With gender assignment, a man who wants to stay home and watch the kids might have confusion about his identity as a man.

With gender assignment, you cut off half of who you are. You say, *Oh, I'm a male humanoid. That means I'm not a female humanoid. That means I'm not a female horse or a male horse, or a female plant or a male plant, or a male piece of carpet or a female piece of carpet.* You receive sexually based on your gender assignment. You refuse to receive from everything around you because it doesn't fit with what you have decided you can receive. You say, *I can only receive from males,* or *I can only receive from females.* What if that were a lie?

What If You Could Receive The Energy Of Everything In The Universe?

What if you could receive the energy of all the plants and animals, all the houses, all the chairs you sit in, and everything else in the universe? What if your life could be a constant state of orgasm?

Going into agreement with your gender assignment is like turning yourself into everything that you are not and making sure that the oneness of you never gets to show up. Fun, huh? How much of your life is actually a simulation of life rather than the truth of it? Have you spent your life judging what you are not, that if you were, would actually give you what you think you want—except that you're never willing to be that because that would mean you would have to give up everything you're not and become everything you are?

Are you actually afraid of who you are? You'll pretend to be somebody, you'll try to be somebody, but you won't actually let all of you show up because you're sure that if you let all of you out, something would go wrong. Something terrible could happen if you actually showed up. That "something terrible" is you—which is far more magnificent than you want to be. Have you ever noticed how much of your life you don't really feel like you're there for?

When you're out in nature, for example, do you feel like you're actually really there? Or when you're having a conversation with a friend, are you really there, conversing?

Consider how much energy it takes to contain an infinite being who has unlimited possibilities and confine it into the puny little life you call your reality. Do you have any idea how much energy it requires for you to keep yourself held down and hidden? No one else can do that to you. Consider for a moment that maybe it's a stupid and insane decision. Maybe you could choose something else.

If you're defining yourself as male or female, you are defining you as a limitation. You are limiting what you can be. If you were being the omnisexualness and the omnipresence and the oneness you truly are, would your gender ever be a limitation? Or would it be a source of pleasure and fun, help you get what you want, and enjoy your life more?

Are you willing to give up all those gender assignments and all the pretenses of what you're supposed to be based on your gender? Are you willing to destroy and uncreate all those limitations, and start claiming and owning all the power of you instead?

You Are Not Really One Gender Or The Other

There isn't any gender you have not been in one lifetime or another. You are actually both male and female right now. You are operating different bodies in different dimensions and realities. Somewhere in time you're still a male or still a female. Recognize that in order to keep this whole simulated reality in existence, you have to think of yourself as only one gender and not the other, and you have to convince yourself of a whole lot of lies like time, space, dimensions and realities.

We're not saying you have to change this, or destroy or uncreate it, we're just pointing out that what you have is not a choice between *this* or *that.* You actually have infinite choice. Would you have a different relationship with some of your female friends or your male friends if you were really living from the point of view of choice rather than gender?

What we're looking to do is to get you to oneness, to the awareness of your life, which is the place you create magic from. When you begin to have an awareness of your life and begin to see how you create your limitations, you can let go of them and create something different.

Chapter Eighteen

The Value of You

Most people spend their lives trying to prove they're valuable, but they're not really willing to see the true value of themselves. They calculate the right and wrong of themselves, the black and white, the positive and negative, the good, the bad and the ugly of themselves. These calculations are based on a mistaken understanding of who they are.

We're sorry. Whatever you may presently think, you are not the good, bad, and the ugly. You are the presence of you. You are the awareness of you. Can you get the difference between the calculations of you and the awareness of you?

Everything that demands that you look for the value of you, rather than having the awareness of you, would you revoke, recant, rescind, reclaim, renounce, destroy and uncreate it please?

Are You Willing To Have The Awareness Of You And Your Contribution?

One day after I (Dain) began facilitating Access classes with Gary, I went into a serious judgment and calculation of my value. I was struck with how thoroughly Gary could perceive and follow the energy of a class, and I said to him,

> "You know, I don't really add any value to you by being up there teaching with you."
> He said, "What?"
> I said, "I don't perceive that I have any value co-facilitating the class. Maybe it would be more valuable if you did it by yourself because I know you can perceive all the energy."
> He said, "No. There are awarenesses I have when you're up there with me."
> I said, "What are you talking about? I can't see that."
> He said, "Well, are you willing to have the awareness of you and your contribution?"
> I said, "No, not at all."
> He asked me again, "Are you willing to have the awareness of you and what you are contributing?"
> And again I said, "Not at all."

Then I realized I was looking for my value. And what is value? Value is always a judgment. It's always relative to something else. It's a relationship and it's always got a judgment attached to it. I was asking myself, *Where do I fit in this relationship?* I was looking for my value in this particular co-facilitation and all I could come up with was judgment.

I started feeling heavy and pathetic.

Gary asked me, "What if you had an awareness of what you are contributing? What if you had an awareness of what is actually going on?"

And suddenly I went, "Oh!" and everything lightened up, because I started looking for awareness instead of judging the value that I had or didn't have. Whenever you look for your value, you always go into a place of judgment—and you generally come up short. You come up with negative reference points and negative judgments of how you're functioning. When you look for your value, you lose your awareness of you, and the awareness of your presence is what's unbelievably valuable.

Looking for your value always involves a comparison, and you spend your life competing with everybody around you. You go into calibration and proof, and you continuously try to prove you have value, rather than knowing you do. You go in search of something you already are. Rather than being aware of yourself and knowing that your presence and contribution to life really exists, you look for your value. You try to prove your value. Ninety-nine percent of the people are trying to prove they are not what they've already decided they are.

You're Great Just The Way You Are

A lot of parents approach their kids with the attitude, *I know you could be much better.* This puts the kids in the position of trying to prove they're better than their parents think they are—which means they're trying to prove they're something they don't think they are.

What we really want parents to tell their kids is, You're great just the way you are. But most parents are saying, *No, you're not great the way you are.* Kids can't see that they have any value, especially to their own family.

The bad part about being a kid is that you come in to make your parents happy. This is utterly impossible, because most parents don't want to be happy. Stop trying to make other people happy. You can't make anybody anything. Only they can make themselves that. Have you judged yourself a failure because you didn't succeed with your parents or someone else? Would you revoke, recant, rescind, reclaim, renounce, destroy and uncreate all that please?

What would it be like if you stopped judging you and tried to find the value of you and recognized the *extraordinariness* of you instead? Assume that we are a consumer report and we're classing you as superior. How does that feel? People who act superior actually feel inferior. That's not what we're talking about. *Superior* is knowing that you are the best car out there; you're the 645 BMW and you're not trying to make yourself into a 1964 VW. Superior comes from an awareness of yourself, not from attempting to prove that you have value.

Please recognize that you are superior when you are being more aware. When you are being aware and present as you, you are truly superior in every way.

Chapter Nineteen

Destroy Yourself Every Day
Create Yourself Every Day

When I (Gary) was thirty years old, I went to Europe for six months. Nobody knew me there. I met new people every day and I created who I was every day. Nobody had a judgment of who I was to hold me in place. Prior to that I had been my parents' child, my dog's owner, so-and-so's friend, somebody's husband, and somebody's father. But I was never me. Who is *me*, anyway? Who am *I*?

You identify yourself as somebody else's something for the majority of your life, but seldom do you get to identify yourself as you. How much of the *you* of you have you eliminated from your life in order to be somebody else's something?

Most of us don't realize that we have no idea of who we really are. We get caught up in certain identities, certain ways of being, certain ideas of whom we are supposed to be, and that's it for the rest of our lives. We don't realize that the I we think we are is actually a creation. What if you destroyed that I and created another?

If you decide that you don't have to function from whom or what you decided you were or weren't yesterday, or what you could be or couldn't be, you can create yourself every day, and your life will start to become the magic and adventure of creation.

The Magic Of Destruction

Most of us don't consider destruction to be something that has the power to move things in the direction we want them to go. We tend to think of creation as something positive and destruction as something negative, but this is not necessarily the case. Sometimes destruction is a terrifically positive force.

Wherever we have decided we have something right in our lives, we stop receiving. We decide, *This area of my life is just fine and I don't need to put any attention on it, and I can forget about it.* As soon as we think we've got the right relationship, the right amount of money, the right property, the right lifestyle, the right anything, we tend to shut down. We only work on what we think is wrong, and we ignore what we think is right. We think, *Okay, I've got this right. I don't have to work on it anymore.* This might sound good, but it creates a limitation.

It's as easy to destroy what is right as it is to destroy what is wrong. And actually, it's a great idea. If you destroy everything in your life every day—if you destroy everything you thought you were yesterday, last week or any other time—it puts you on the creative edge of your life every day.

When you start destroying those things, you're refusing to function from the same place you were the day before. It's one of the easiest and most effective ways of beginning to live in the question. You can approach it this way: *Okay, if I were born today in this body, at this age, what would I choose? What would I choose if I had no past?*

You get to destroy everything that you made significant about the past, everything you made real, everything you made solid, and simply ask yourself, What would I like today? What would be really cool to have show up today?

Are You Willing To Destroy Your Life As It Currently Exists?

Are you willing to destroy your life as it currently exists? That can be a pretty frightening question for a lot of people, especially when we tell them that what they have to destroy are the parts of their lives they think they have right. Those are the parts most people refuse to destroy—but it's exactly those places you have to destroy so the magic of you can start to show up. Which is more important? To be magic or to be secure in what you think you have right? Will you choose to have the magic and give up the rightness of your points of view? Are you willing to destroy your life as it currently exists?

Every night when you go to bed, say, *Everything I believed I was and everything I created today, I destroy and uncreate it all. Who I was today, I destroy and uncreate.* Doing this doesn't mean you lose your talents and abilities. It means you open the door to more talents and greater abilities.

People say things like, "I'm too old to start over." Now there's a fixed point of view. Have you decided you're too old to start over creating yourself? Would you like to give that up now?

When we coach performers, people are always amazed at how quickly they get better. In two to five minutes people make truly significant changes. It takes a very short period of time to improve. How is this done? We work with them to destroy and uncreate their fixed points of view about what they thought they could do. When you destroy and uncreate your fixed points of view about what you think you can be, do, have, create and generate, then a whole new you shows up that's far greater than anything you ever thought was possible.

That's when life gets fun. You wake up in the morning and ask, Okay, who the heck am I today? You have no clue. You get to create who you are each day. Can you imagine waking up every day like that? Who am I today?

At the end of each day, you can say, *Everything I was today, I now destroy and uncreate.* In the morning when you wake up, you get to ask, *"Okay, who the hell am I today and what grand and glorious adventure am I going to have?"* When you do this, you turn your life into an adventure instead of drudgery. The humdrum world goes away when you destroy and uncreate everything every night and in the morning ask, *"Okay, who am I today and what grand and glorious adventure am I going to have?"* You are creating you—brand new.

Tomorrow Has A Possibility
For Being Even Greater

Remember to destroy everything at the end of the great days as well as at the end of the crappy days. Realize *great* and *crappy* are judgments—that's a story for another time—but regardless of what the day was for you, destroy it. When you destroy you at the end of a great day, tomorrow has a possibility for being even greater.

Note to Readers

Access is an energy transformation program which links seasoned wisdom, ancient knowledge and channeled energies with highly contemporary motivational tools. Its purpose is to set you free by giving you access to your truest, highest self.

The information, tools and techniques presented in this book are just a small taste of what Access has to offer. There is a whole universe of Access processes and classes.

If there are places where you can't get things in your life to work the way you know they ought to, you might be interested in attending an Access class or workshop or locating an Access facilitator, who can work with you to give you greater clarity about issues you can't overcome. Access processes are done with a trained facilitator and are based on the energy of you and the person you're working with.

For more information, visit:
www.accessconsciousness.com

Glossary

Bars

The bars are a hands-on Access process that involves a light touch upon the head to contact points that correspond to different aspects of one's life. There are points for joy, sadness, body and sexuality, awareness, kindness, gratitude, peace and calm. There is even a money bar. These points are called bars because they run from one side of the head to the other.

Be

In this book, the word be is sometimes used to refer to you, the infinite being you truly be, as opposed to a contrived point of view about who you think you are.

Clearing Statement (POD/POC)

The clearing statement we use in Access is: Right and wrong, good and bad, POD, POC, all nine, shorts, boys and beyonds.™

Right and wrong, good and bad is shorthand for: What's good, perfect and correct about this? What's wrong, mean, vicious, terrible, bad and awful about this? What's right and wrong, good and bad?

POC is the point of creation of the thoughts, feelings and emotions immediately preceding whatever you decided.

POD is the point of destruction immediately preceding whatever you decided. It's like pulling the bottom card out of a house of cards. The whole thing falls down.

All nine stands for nine layers of crap that were taken out. You know that somewhere in those nine layers, there's got to be a pony because you couldn't put that much shit in one place without having a pony in there. It's shit that you're generating yourself, which is the bad part.

Shorts is the short version of: What's meaningful about this? What's meaningless about this? What's the punishment for this? What's the reward for this?

Boys stands for nucleated spheres. Have you ever seen one of those kids' bubble pipes? Blow here and you create a mass of bubbles. You pop one bubble and the other bubbles fill in the space

Beyonds are feelings or sensations you get that stop your heart, stop your breath, or stop your willingness to look at possibilities. It's like when your business is in the red and you get another final notice and you say argh! You weren't expecting that right now.

Sometimes, instead of saying "use the clearing statement," we just say, "POD and POC it."

Other Books

The Place
By Gary M. Douglas

As Jake Rayne travels through Idaho in his classic 57 Thunderbird, a devastating accident is the catalyst for a journey he isn't expecting. Alone in the deep forest, with his body shattered and broken, Jake calls out for help. The help that finds him changes not only his life but his whole reality. Jake is opened up to the awareness of possibilities; possibilities that we have always known should be but that have not yet shown up. A Barnes and Noble Best Seller.

Being You, Changing the World
By Dr. Dain Heer

Have you always known that something COMPLETELY DIFFERENT is possible? What if you had a handbook for infinite possibilities and dynamic change to guide you? With tools and processes that actually worked and invited you to a completely different way of being? For you? And the world?

Divorceless Relationships
By Gary M. Douglas

What if you don't have to divorce you in order to create an intimate relationship? This book contains tools, exercises and processes you can use so you do not have to give up any part of yourself in a relationship.

Money Isn't the Problem. You Are.
By Gary M. Douglas & Dr. Dain Heer

Offering out-of-the-box concepts with money. It's not about money. It never is. It's about what you're willing to receive.

Talk to the Animals
By Gary M. Douglas & Dr. Dain Heer

Did you know that every animal, every plant, every structure on this planet has consciousness and desires to gift to you? Animals have a tremendous amount of information and amazing gifts they can give to us if we are willing to receive them.

Sex is Not a Four Letter Word but Relationship Often Times Is
By Gary M. Douglas & Dr. Dain Heer

Funny , frank, and delightfully irreverent, this book offers readers an entirely fresh view of how to create great intimacy and exceptional sex. What if you could stop guessing—and find out what REALLY works?

Right Riches for You!
By Gary M. Douglas & Dr. Dain Heer

What if generating money and having money were fun and joyful? What if, in having fun and joy with money, you receive more of it? What would that be like? Money follows joy; joy does not follow money. As seen on Lifetime Television's Balancing Act Show.

About the Authors

Gary M. Douglas

The illustrious best-selling author and international speaker, Gary Douglas, pioneered a set of transformational life changing tools and processes known as Access Consciousness® over 20 years ago. These cutting edge tools have transformed the lives of thousands of people all over the world. In fact, his work has spread to  47 countries, with 2,000 trained facilitators worldwide. Simple but so effective, the tools facilitate people of all ages and backgrounds to help remove limitations holding them back from a full life.

Gary was born in Midwest USA and raised in San Diego, California. Although he came from a *"normal"* middle class family, he was fascinated from an early age with the human psyche and this interest grew into a desire to assist people to *"know what they know"* and expand into more awareness, joy and abundance.

These pragmatic tools he has developed are not only being used by celebrities, corporates and teachers but also by health professionals (psychologists, chiropractors, naturopaths) to improve the health & wellbeing of their clients.

Prior to creating Access Consciousness® Gary Douglas was a successful realtor in Santa Barbara, California and also completed a psychology degree. Although he attained material wealth and was regarded as *"successful,"* his life began to lack meaning and so he began his search to find a new way forward- one that would create change in the world and in people's lives.

Gary is the author of 8 books including the best selling novel *"The Place."* He describes the inspiration behind the writing, *"I wanted to explore the possibilities for how life could be. To allow people to know there actually is no necessity to live with the ageing, insanity, stupidity, intrigue, violence, craziness, trauma and drama we live with, as though we have no choice. "The Place" is about people knowing that all things are possible. Choice is the source of creation. What if our choices can be changed in an instant? What if we could make choice more real than the decisions and stuck points we buy as real?"*

Gary has an incredible level of awareness and care for all living things, *"I would like people be more aware and more conscious and to realize we need to be stewards of the earth not users and abusers of the earth. If we start to see the possibilities of what we have available to us, instead of trying to create our piece of the pie, we could create a different world."*

A vibrant 70-year-old grandfather (*who is almost "ageless"*) with a very different view on life, Gary believes we are here to express our uniqueness and experience the ease and joy of living. He continues to inspire others, teaching across the world and making a massive contribution to the planet. He openly proclaims that for him, *"life is just beginning."*

Gary also has a wide range of personal and other business interests. These include: a passion for antiques (*Gary established "The Antique Guild" in Brisbane, Australia in 2012*) riding spirited stallions and breeding Costarricense De Paso horses, and an eco retreat in Costa Rica set to open in 2014.

To find out more, please visit:
www.GaryMDouglas.com
www.AccessConsciousness.com
www.Costarricense-Paso.com

Dr. Dain Heer

Dr. Dain Heer is an international speaker, author and facilitator of advanced Access Consciousness® workshops worldwide. His unique and transforming points of view on bodies, money, future, sex and relationships transcend everything currently being taught.

Dr. Heer invites and inspires people to greater conscious awareness from total allowance, caring, humor and a deep inner knowing.

Dr. Heer started work as a Network Chiropractor back in 2000 in California, USA. He came across Access Consciousness® at a point in his life when he was deeply unhappy and even planning suicide.

When none of the other modalities and techniques Dr. Heer had been studying were giving him lasting results or change, Access Consciousness® changed everything for him and his life began to expand and grow with more ease and speed than even he could have imagined possible.

Dr. Heer now travels the world facilitating classes and has developed a unique energy process for change for individuals and groups, called The Energetic Synthesis of Being. He has a completely different approach to healing by teaching people to tap into and recognize their own abilities and knowing. The energetic transformation possible is fast—and truly dynamic.

To find out more, please visit:
www.DrDainHeer.com
www.BeingYouChangingTheWorld.com
www.BeingYouClass.com

About Access Consciousness®

Access Consciousness® is an energy transformation program which links seasoned wisdom, ancient knowledge and channeled energies with highly contemporary motivational tools. Its purpose is to set you free by giving you access to your truest, highest self.

The purpose of Access is to create a world of consciousness and oneness. Consciousness includes everything and judges nothing. It is our target to facilitate you to the point where you receive awareness of everything with no judgment of anything. If you have no judgment of anything, then you get to look at everything for what it is, not for what you want it to be, not for what it ought to be, but just for what it is.

Consciousness is the ability to be present in your life in every moment, without judgment of you or anyone else. It is the ability to receive everything, reject nothing, and create everything you desire in life—greater than what you currently have, and more than what you can imagine.

What if you were willing to nurture and care for you?

What if you would open the doors to being everything you have decided it is not possible to be?

What would it take for you to realize how crucial you are to the possibilities of the world?

The information, tools and techniques presented in this book are just a small taste of what Access Consciousness® has to offer. There is a whole Universe of processes and classes.

If there are places where you can't get things in your life to work the way you know they ought to, then you might be interested in attended an Access Consciousness® class, workshop or locating a facilitator. They can work with you to give you greater clarity about issues you haven't yet overcome.

Access Consciousness® processes are done with a trained facilitator, and are based on the energy of you and the person you're working with.

Come and explore more at:
www.AccessConsciousness.com

Access Seminars And Classes

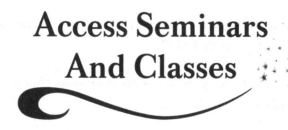

If you liked what you read in this book and are interested in attended Access seminars, workshops or classes, then for a very different point of view, read-on and sample a taste of what is available.

Access Bars (One Day)

Facilitated by Certified Access Bars Facilitators worldwide, Bars is one of the foundational tools of Access. In this one day class, you will learn a hands-on energetic process, which you will gift and receive during the class. The Access Bars are 32 points on the head that when lightly touched clear all of the limitations you have about different areas of your life and body. This areas include money, aging, body, sexuality, joy, sadness, healing, creativity, awareness and control plus many more. What would it be like to have more freedom in all of these areas? In this one day class you will learn the basic tools of Access Consciousness® and receive and gift 2 Access Bars sessions. At worst it will feel like a great massage and at best your whole life will change!

Prerequisites: None
Facilities by Certified Access Facilitators Worldwide

Access Foundation (Two Day)

This two day class is about giving you the space to look at your life as a different possibility. Unlock your limitations about emobdiment, finances, success, relationships, family, YOU and your capacities, and much more! Step into greater possibilities for having everything you truly desire in life as you learn tools and questions to change anything that's not working for you.

Prerequisites: Access Bars
Facilitated by Certified Access Facilitators Worldwide

Access, Level 1 (Two Day)

This is a two day class that shows you how to be more conscious in every area of your life and gives you practical tools that allow you to continue expanding this in your day-to-day! Create a phenomenal life filled with magic, joy and ease and clear your limitations about what is truly available for you. Discover the 5 Elements of Intimacy, create energy flows, start laughing and celebrating living and practice a hands-on body process that has created miraculous results all over the world!

Prerequisites: Access Foundation
Facilitated Exclusively by Gary M. Douglas and Dr. Dain Heer

Access, Levels 2 & 3 (Four Day)

Having completed Level I and opened up to more awareness of you, you start to have more choice in life and become aware of what choice truly is. This four day class covers a huge range of areas including the joy of business, living life for the fun of it, no fear, courage and leadership, changing the molecular structure of things, creating your body and your sexual reality, and how to stop holding on to what you want to get rid of! Is it time to start receiving the change you've been asking for?

Prerequisites: Access Bars, Foundation, and Level I
Facilitated Exclusively by Gary M. Douglas and Dr. Dain Heer

The Energetic Synthesis of Being - ESB (Three Day)

This three day class is a unique way of working with energy, groups of people and their bodies simultaneously, created and facilitated by Dr. Dain Heer. During this class, your being, your body and the earth are invited to energetically synthesize in a way that creates a more conscious life and a more conscious planet. You begin to access and be energies you never knew were available. By being these energies, by being you, you change everything; the planet, your life and everyone you come into contact with. What else is possible then?

Prerequisites: Access Bars, Foundation and Level I, II, & III
Facilitated Exclusively by Dr. Dain Heer

Access Body Class (Two Day)

During this two day class you will learn verbal processes and hands on bodywork that unlock the tension, resistance, and disease of the body. Do you have a talent and ability to work with bodies that you haven't yet unlocked? Are you a body worker (massage therapist, chiropractor, medical doctor, nurse) looking for a way to enhance the healing you can do for your clients? Come play with us and begin to explore how to communicate and relate to bodies, including yours, in a whole new way.

Prerequisites: Access Bars
Facilitated by Access Body Class Facilitators Worldwide.

Connect With Access Online

www.AccessConciousness.com
www.GaryMDouglas.com
www.DrDainHeer.com
www.BeingYouChangingtheWorld.com

www.YouTube.com/drdainheer
www.Facebook.com/drdainheer
www.Twitter.com/drdainheer

www.Facebook.com/accessconsciousness
www.RightRecoveryForYou.com
www.AccessTrueKnowledge.com